D1297080

ADDRESSES OF
JOHN HAY

John Hay

ADDRESSES OF JOHN HAY

Essay Index Reprint Series

BOOKS FOR LIBRARIES PRESS
FREEPORT, NEW YORK

First Published 1906
Reprinted 1970

INTERNATIONAL STANDARD BOOK NUMBER:
0-8369-1755-3

LIBRARY OF CONGRESS CATALOG CARD NUMBER:
77-121477

PRINTED IN THE UNITED STATES OF AMERICA

CONTENTS

CONTENTS

FRANKLIN IN FRANCE

PREPARED FOR THE MERCHANTS' CLUB OF CHICAGO, DECEMBER, 1904, BUT NOT DELIVERED, OWING TO THE DEATH OF A BROTHER OF MR. HAY. PUBLISHED IN *THE CENTURY MAGAZINE* FOR JANUARY, 1906

FRANKLIN IN FRANCE

WHEN the men of the Revolution threw into the game of war their lives, their fortunes, and their sacred honor, they meant to stand by their solemn professions. They intended to fight the battle out—to stand or fall with the principles they had announced. They were ready for death and defeat, but they were resolved on life and victory. They held success to be their immediate duty. They were not greedy of glory; they wanted liberty. And they were anxious to gain this inestimable good in the quickest possible way. They cast their eyes over-seas to search for what help might come from abroad. If there was among the nations of Europe a sense of wrong, a jealousy, or an antipathy to England which might be useful to their cause, a motive of interest, a spirit of gain, which might be caught and set to work for the new and struggling freedom, they were ready to use them. The gnomes working for the heroes was a well-worn myth. They knew they were fighting the battle of the human race. Let the human race lend a hand, if it would.

So, one of the early acts of the Continental Congress was to form a secret committee to correspond with friends abroad. It was composed of five members, Benjamin Franklin, John Jay, Thomas Johnson, John Dickinson, and Benjamin Harrison—names we all recognize yet. The committee was a strong one. Franklin was the most skilled diplomatist in the colonies, by natural aptness and by technical experience. So the bulk of the work naturally devolved upon him. He began correpondence with British Liberals, Dutch Lawyers, French Doctors, and Spanish Princes. It took at least six months to exchange letters between Paris and Philadelphia. We can now scarcely imagine the sickening weariness of hope deferred in those days.

To France, as the traditional enemy of England, all eyes were naturally turned. Mr. Jay relates a singular incident, which powerfully impressed many minds, of an old gentleman who arrived in Philadelphia in 1775, and offered to the Congress then in session, in good Parisian English, the assistance of the King of France, in stores, arms, ammunition, and money. Being asked for his name, credentials, and other ambassadorial baggage, he drew his hand across his throat and said politely but positively, "Gentlemen, I shall take care of my head." No tombstone was ever more discreet than this old gentleman. He disappeared the next day from Philadelphia, and took such good care of his head that the keenest-scented annalists have never discovered a trace of him. If we were inclined to be superstitious, the only two circumstances we know of him—his Parisian accent and his tender care of his head—might induce us to take him for St. Denis. This and other incidents made men think and talk much of France. No letters came from Franklin's correspondents. The committee resolved to send an ambassador to France; and a candidate turned up the moment he was wanted—Silas Deane, of Connecticut.

It is a curious fact, and one which shows how our nation sprang at once fully developed into being, that our first foreign minister was a defeated member of Congress. A quiet legation is the stuffed mattress which the political acrobat wants always to see ready under him in case of a slip.

Silas Deane sailed to France and soon set on foot very extensive business operations for the assistance of the colonies. With the aid of that strange mixture of charlatanry and genius, Caron de Beaumarchais, he sent a large quantity of valuable stores to America, and a small quantity of worthless officers. He had the favor and the secret assistance of the court. The virtuous and far-seeing Turgot, who knew there was much to lose and little to gain by the American alliance, after protesting in vain against the Beaumarchais interest, had been dismissed the cabinet. The Comte de Vergennes assisted the colonies privately with one hand, and with the other dexterously stroked the right way the fur of the irritated British lion.

It was thought best, however, that stronger hands should take charge of this business. On September 26, 1776, Congress elected an embassy to France, consisting of its two most illustrious names. The choice of Franklin and Jefferson shows how vital the French alliance had come to be considered. Jefferson declined. Congress elected in his place Arthur Lee of Virginia. Mr. Deane was also retained in the embassy.

When Franklin was elected in secret session he turned to Dr. Rush and said in shopman's phrase, "I am an old remnant—you may have me for what you please." He was seventy years old and the most famous American of that day. He sailed in the swift sloop of war *Reprisal,* Captain Wickes, which captured two prizes on the way; and about six weeks later he descended at the Hotel de Hambourg, in the Latin Quarter. I dined there once, for Franklin's sake. I hope the kitchen was better in his day.

It was a wonderful France that he found. The old dispensation was drawing nigh its end, and no one dreamed it. The new daylight was dawning and the darkness comprehended it not. The best king of his race was sitting on his thorny throne, doing, according to his feeble lights, his best for the people who should one day slay him. Over his weak head were gathering the storms that had been brewing for centuries. His ancestors had eaten the sour grapes of tyranny, and his innocent teeth were set on edge.

Through long ages of wrong and rapine and murder this great, patient France had submitted to its masters. These are not phrases. The kings and great lords robbed and killed their vassals with no thought of accountability. It was not a hundred years since the young Prince Charolais invented that humorous amusement of shooting tilers on the roofs of houses and seeing them roll and tumble into the street—from mere gaiety of heart, says the chronicler. Still in many parts of France that odious right of *seigneurie* was retained, which made peasant husbands loathe the face of their first-born. And everywhere there was no right of the poor that the rich man greatly respected. There was no feeling of the plebeian which the noble thought worth caring for. The monarchy was still the most splendid of Europe. The court was more brilliant than anything the world will ever see again. There was an appearance of wealth and movement in the great cities. But in the fields there was gaunt famine and dull, hopeless misery. D'Argenson says that in 1738, an era cited as one of peace and prosperity, "men died thick as flies, in poverty and eating the grass of the fields." Rank had prepared its own destruction by its crimes. Its part in the play was over. The groans of suffering humanity were not yet heard, but of God. He would take care of his little ones in due time.

This vast French monarchy was undermined. The enormous power, built up with labor and pain by a long line of kings from Charlemagne to Louis le Grand, was gone: not the less utterly gone that no one saw it go, and no one had as yet marked its absence. It had grown by fitful though continual advances through the English wars of the Charleses, plucking always prerogative from the bloody fields of disaster. It had grown stout and plethoric, fed with blood and nourished with crimes by that quaint and pious knave, Louis XI. Before he died it was out of its nonage, and it flourished on without much effort on the part of the subsequent kings. In the reign of Louis XIV it reached its acme. So great a king as Louis never lived. Yet he was the most commonplace of men, were he not king. His reign was glorious, people say. That is, a great army and able generals, whom he let alone, fought frightful and useless battles which impoverished France and gained nothing. He encouraged arts and literature, by giving to Molière and Racine, and the rest of those Titans, about the same distinction and favor which he would have given to a clever dancing-master. He built Versailles. This is the masterpiece, the outward manifestation of the consummate bloom, of European king-craft. This stupendous work was the last great effort of the royal prerogative—the last great enterprise which a king has undertaken without at least attempting to persuade the people that it was for their benefit. But this vast pile and these lordly pleasure-grounds say cynically to the world, "The King is the State." Monarchy has never recovered from the strain of that effort. It is the infallible symptom of decadence in a man or a government when it undertakes works which cannot pay expenses. The Pharaohs perished when their Pyramids were finished. Napoleon went to Moscow to meet his evil genius. Every country town in America has the ruins of a fine house called somebody's "Folly."

This great King Louis died in a miserable old age, and they carted him off to St. Denis with small ceremony, and his great-grandson, Louis XV, reigned in his stead. But the regent of Orléans ruled over France in the babyhood of the King. We know what this candid prince thought of his own rule. He said one day to the Abbé Du Bois, his prime minister, "A devil of a kingdom, this—governed by a sot and a pander!" A good-natured man, this Duke of Orléans, thoroughly corrupt, with good intentions that were never fulfilled, with amiable qualities that led to nothing but shames and crimes. Breathing a poisoned air from his birth, moral health was impossible to him. He meant well to the people, but his vampires drew their blood and coined it to supply those mad revels of the Palais Royal that our decent age refuses to describe. His reign served to grade the passage from the Fourteenth to the Fifteenth Louis.

And here the last word of the monarchy is indeed said. When a king like Louis XV becomes possible, then the world begins to ask whether it may not get on without kings. The life of this unspeakably mean creature seems meant to show us how questionable is any system that may sometime give to utter depravity a practical omnipotence of mischief. There may have been others as licentious, as cowardly, as cruel, as false, as avaricious as he. But no other man could set these sordid vices up in the sight of the world, and by the accursed alchemy of power turn them to graces and examples to be praised and followed by all who were weakly loyal or meanly servile. This was the work of Louis the Well-beloved. He rolled in the garbage of vice so that the purple could hardly be clean again. He depraved and corrupted the court, so that from the courtier class nothing more was to be hoped. You would not pardon me if I should give you a catalogue of his enormous and cowardly crimes. One who reads attentively the memoirs of those times comes back as from a visit to a charnel-house. The tone of levity in which these horrors are recorded is the most saddening thing. This man was so flattered and fawned upon that his conscience went to sleep disgusted, and he really thought he was rather a good sort of fellow.

That he might play out his part to the end he was granted robust health and long life. His last sin found him out, and he crowned a despicable life by a loathsome death. He was riding in the park and he saw a peasant's funeral go by. He rode up and asked who was dead. He turned pale at the answer—it was the name of his last victim. But some dreadful fascination induced him to question again. What did she die of? "Smallpox, sire!" Gasping for horror, he dashed away to the palace and lay down to die. Carlyle has drawn with the unpitying hand of an avenging angel the scenes of that unedifying death-bed. The polluted soul broke loose at last, and sped away to its own place. The church blessed the parting. We will try to be charitable, too; but we are irresistibly reminded of one of the few bitter things that Franklin ever said: "If such souls escape, it is not worth while to keep a devil."

The courtiers rushed to congratulate Louis XVI and Marie Antoinette on their accession to the throne. But they fell on their knees and said: "Help us, O God! We are too young to govern."

It was a true presentiment that saddened for

the youthful and virtuous monarch this first moment of power. He did not see, as we do, the full extent of the monstrous debt that monarchy owed to the moral equilibrium. He did not fully appreciate the deplorable state of his realm, in finance, in agriculture, in every incident of national life. Least of all did he understand the mighty power of public opinion, which had been stealthily gaining ground through the last two reigns. A power had grown up never contemplated by earlier kings.

A race of audacious thinkers had arisen—a modern growth for France. Under the great Louis, literature was encouraged, as cooking was, as music was, as tailoring was, to add to the splendor of the court. But under the Regency the new spirit came to light. The Regent loved letters for their own sake. He had a sentimental love for freedom, even; and if he had not been a Bourbon he might himself have been a patriot. Under him began that powerful impulse of research and philosophical speculation that continued amid neglect or impotent, fitful persecution under the reign of Louis XV and reached its lordly stature and attained its predestined purpose in the wreck and chaos of the Revolution.

The first conspicuous name among those who led the van of this great intellectual movement was Montesquieu, who began at twenty by writing an argument against the eternal damnation of the heathen, and through a long and busy life sent forth, in rapid succession, those bold and brilliant disquisitions that opened to the mind of France a vastly wider horizon of political speculation than ever had been dreamed of before. His "Spirit of Laws" alone ranks him with those great original geniuses that clasp hands in spirit across the gulf of ages. He was the earliest of the philosophers. He shines almost sole in his generation, clear as the morning star, unconscious of the red tumult of the coming dawn. Then came Voltaire, who ran with that lightning-flash of intuition through the whole cycle of letters and science and politics, finding nothing good or venerable, touching with the Ithuriel spear of wit and logic every department of human affairs, and discovering everywhere only hopeless disease—as the wild humor caught him, now mocking like a fiend, now weeping like a pitying angel; and Diderot, with his great genius and incomplete character, his gigantic schemes and his little life, his mighty collaborators in the Encyclopedia, d'Alembert, de Prades, Dumarsais, and the incomparable Turgot, whose genius and virtue shine together, a beacon in those dark days—all these, working confusedly, without plan, were building up that vast edifice of public opinion which was to harbor and protect the free thought of the century.

Never before had there been seen such activity in the natural sciences. Buffon and Malesherbes were busy plucking its mystery out from the heart of nature.

In the world of metaphysics there was a vast and restless energy, with results always more disheartening. Condillac deduced all moral and mental phenomena from sensation. Helvetius, adopting the theories of Condillac, went mercilessly through to atheism and pure selfishness. The age was so corrupt, they cynically hailed this theory of absolute selfishness as the new gospel and cried, "This man has told everybody's secret. (*"C'est un homme qui a dit le secret de tout le monde."*)

The mind of the world seemed dropping into mere materialism, when a shabby fellow came to Paris and spoke a word that the world was vaguely waiting for. This was Jean Jacques Rousseau, who, weak, wicked, half mad as he was, demonstrated the impotence and barrenness of this materialist philosophy, and prepared, more than any other, the minds of men for the reception of the wild evangel of the Revolution. There was never a shabbier prophet sent on earth, but the lesson he taught was simple and necessary. He recalled to the world what the wits had forgotten—that there are such facts as God, and love, and liberty.

Floating at random in the writings of that century, we find scraps of prophecy not half understood by their authors and not at all by the world. Leibnitz said in 1704 that a revolution was coming by which the great would lose and the world profit. Chesterfield said (1753), "Before the end of this century the trades of king and priest will lose half their value." D'Argenson in 1739, in his great treatise on decentralization, practically eliminated the aristocracy,—aristocrat though he was,—calling them the drones of the hive, and enunciated the sublime doctrine that, though equality was impossible, it should be the aim of all governments to attain it. Voltaire said in 1764, with the dim regret of an old prophet who should not see the coming of the rosy footsteps on the mountains of the future, "Young men are lucky—they will see fine things." But Diderot came nearest the true spirit of the Pythoness possessed when he said in 1774, "The public execution of a king will change the spirit of a nation forever."

These utterances sound startlingly clear and distinct to us after the fact. But then they were voices crying in the wilderness, and the world, if it heard them at all, smiled indulgently and tapped its wise forehead. Countless vague and indistinct systems of government had been shaped in philosophic garrets. But of late young men had begun to study constitutions—the Greek, the Roman, the English, and, later, those almost perfect specimens of statecraft afforded by the constitutions of the American Colonies, which were styled by Tom Paine the grammar of politics. They were to liberty what grammar is to language, defining its parts of speech and practically constructing them into syntax. The tempest in America was manifestly shaping the current of free thought in France. Thus did our nation, even in its godlike babyhood, teach the doctors in the temple of liberty.

I have delayed you some time with this résumé of the state of thought and opinion in France at the arrival of Franklin, but I think you would pardon me if you knew how much I had rejected. It seemed necessary to say this much to explain in some measure the immediate and enormous popularity that greeted the American envoy. The world of pomp and glitter and tradition had in reality passed away. The age of ideas had dawned. To the sight of the world Franklin came as the agent of certain revolted colonies of England to seek material aid to sustain the hard-pushed rebellion. But to the enlightened eye of history he is an envoy from the New World to the Old, addressing to its half-awakened heart and conscience the soul-stirring invitation to be free. No fitter choice was ever made by any nation in any age. There was too heavy a sea running to have any incompetence on the quarter-deck.

An interest which we can scarcely comprehend was taken in that day in natural science. Franklin was, by universal consent, the greatest natural philosopher of his time. He was hailed as the confidant of nature—the playmate of the lightning, a Prometheus unpunished. The brightest constructive and critical energies of the best minds were devoted to the solution of political problems. And here, they said, was a man who had founded many states upon the principles of abstract justice, and had consolidated them at last into a superb model republic. For this hasty generalization had seized the foreign mind, always too apt to regard leaders instead of masses, and it was long before the millions of Americans got their due abroad.

Thus it came that the great heart of liberal France went out at once in a quick rush of welcome to Franklin. He was the point that attracted the overcharged electricity of that vast and stormy mass of active thought. He became the talk of the town. They made songs about him. They published more than one hundred and fifty engravings of him, so that his fur cap and spectacles became as familiar as the face of the King on the louis d'or. The pit rose when he entered a theater. These are not trivial details. Those spontaneous honors, paid to an alien citizen by a people so long the victims of degrading tutelage, showed the progress they had made toward liberty. In honoring him they honored themselves. They vaguely felt he was fighting their battle. They read in his serene and noble countenance the promise of better times.

He lived in free and generous style, in a fine house in Passy, to your right as you may have stood in Exhibition years on the ramp of the Trocadéro and looked over the flashing Seine at the Festival of Peace in the Field of Mars. The company one met there was the best in France—the true élite; that is to say, elect. I will give you a few of their names: La Rochefoucauld, Morellet, Buffon, Turgot, Malesherbes, d'Alembert, Condorcet, d'Holbach, Cabanis, Necker, Mirabeau. I utter only names, yet how each starts a spirit! These men, princes all by intellect and many of them by birth, were proud of the friendship of Franklin. I must mention one curiously characteristic expression of Ralph

Izard, who was taken by Congress from the bosom of one of the first families of South Carolina, and sent as minister to Tuscany. He accepted the mission as readily as did in our times a defeated Western senator who, on receiving a despatch from an old public functionary whose name has escaped everybody's memory,—"Will you accept the mission to Bogota?"—replied in five minutes by lightning, "Of course I will. Where the capital D *is* Bogota?" Mr. Izard never found out where Tuscany was, but spent some years in Paris in geographical studies. He was at Franklin's, one evening, in the company I have mentioned, and said sneeringly, "Why could n't we have some of the *gentlemen* of France?" What a faithful forerunner of Preston Brooks!—except that slavery had seventy-five years longer to elaborate Brooks, and so produced a more finished work.

It is needless to say that the adulation which Franklin received did not injure him. Honest praise never hurt any one. It is only men who are meanly flattered that are ruined by it. He went energetically about his work.

For a year his position as envoy was unrecognized by the court, but none the less the French government paid the greatest deference to his representations. Frequent flittings to and from Versailles to Passy; numerous mysterious interviews in Franklin's library with M. Gérard of the Foreign Office (afterward minister to the United States), usually ending in a fresh shipment of arms to America by the sympathetic firm of Hortalez & Co., or a replenishing of the exhausted exchequer of the colonies. The mystery which hung about the firm of Hortalez & Co. has never been wholly cleared; though now it appears that Beaumarchais—the immortal creator of Figaro—was Hortalez, Beaumarchais was the company and the shareholders and the board of directors of that public-spirited firm. The French government seems to have been the rock from which, on Franklin's periodical smiting, gushed forth the streams that kept the mill of Hortalez in motion. But the secrecy necessary to throw dust in the wide-awake eyes of the English ambassador was in the end the cause of woes unnumbered to Beaumarchais. He lived to appreciate in bankruptcy and ruin the serpent-toothed ingratitude of two republics.

The French government, true to the ruinous policy of that day, omitted no effort to cripple England by secretly aiding the colonies; but while the issue of the war remained doubtful, they held aloof from open alliance. The position of our diplomacy abroad seemed almost hopeless at one moment, when Lord Howe was in Philadelphia and a clever young officer named André was quartered in Franklin's house, amusing himself with the philosopher's electrical apparatus, and contenting himself, for all loot on departing, with the sage's picture.

It may amuse some of you who were made merry by Mr. Seward's famous sixty days' reprieves to our late rebellion, to know that Franklin used in Paris a thousand times the same expressions as those by which the sage of Auburn quieted from time to time the semi-rebel diplomatic corps at Washington. He never lost heart, however gloomy the situation. He called our disasters blessings in disguise, and when asked one day if Howe had really captured Philadelphia, he answered, "No. Philadelphia has captured Howe."

This was the dark hour. But it passed, and the first streak of day was the news of the surrender of General Burgoyne. The war was not half over, but its issue was certain from that day. Only the blind obstinacy of the King of England could have protracted it to such brutal and bloody lengths. The French Jupiter saw that the Yankee wagoner was himself getting out of the mire, and so concluded to give him a serious lift. The treaties of alliance and of amity and commerce between France and the United States were signed on February 6, 1778.

It was the sunburst to the colonies after a troubled dawn. The tattered and frost-bitten soldiers of Valley Forge were paraded to receive the joyful news, and the army of the republic shouted, "Long live the King of France!" Washington issued a general order saying it had "pleased the Almighty Ruler of the universe propitiously to defend the cause of the United American States, and by finally raising up a powerful friend among the nations of the earth to establish our liberty and independence upon a lasting foundation." The act of France gave us a standing abroad which we had hitherto lacked. A man's character is made by himself; his reputation exists in the minds of others. Our Declaration asserted our independence, the French alliance proved it. Even before 1776 we were a nation; but until our treaties with France the world regarded us as a rebellion.

This first great act of our diplomacy was as dignified in form as it was valuable in substance. The struggling transatlantic revolt met the proudest monarchy of Europe on terms of absolute equality. By a strange equation of prophecy, the negotiators seemed to recognize the possibilities of the crescent republic and the waning dynasty. "There shall be a firm, inviolable, and universal peace and a true and sincere friendship between the Most Christian King, his heirs and successors, and the United States of America." There is no note of patronage or subservience in these words, nor in these: "If war should break out between France and Great Britain during the continuance of the present war between the United States and England, his Majesty and the said United States shall make it a common cause, and aid each other mutually with their good offices, their counsels, and their forces, according to the exigence of conjunctures, as becomes good and faithful allies. . . . Neither of the two parties shall conclude either truce or peace with Great Britain without the formal consent of the other first obtained; and they mutually engage not to lay down their arms until the independence of the United States shall have been formally or tacitly assured by the treaty or treaties that shall terminate the war."

The effect of the treaty was immediate and most important. Even before it was made public, the rumor of it powerfully affected the courts of the world. Lord North introduced into the House of Commons proposals for conciliation which, if they had been presented in time, would have been gladly accepted by the colonies; but the water had passed by the mill. The American Congress promptly rejected these belated propositions. The British ambassador quitted Paris in justifiable anger; war ensued between England and France. On February 13, 1778, in the harbor of Brest, Paul Jones, in the *Ranger,* had the satisfaction of seeing the American flag saluted for the first time by the guns of a foreign power.

The American navy was born and entered at once on its career of glory. The battle under the starlight between the *Bonhomme Richard* and the *Serapis* set a standard of heroism which may always be emulated but never excelled. In the summer of July, 1778, a stately fleet, under Count d'Estaing, brought to America the first French minister and four thousand troops. Spain joined France against England, through no sympathy with the colonies, but in pursuance of her European policy. And the final harvest of the French alliance was gathered in the crowning victory at Yorktown.

More than a year before, Franklin had been received with joyous enthusiasm by the people of France—for the French people had already come into existence. Now the court was to have the privilege of knowing him. Immediately after the signing of the treaty, he was presented at Versailles and took the palace by storm. One of those trifling chroniclers so dear to the readers of history tells us that he went without the flowing wig required by the full dress of those days. It was not an act of audacity, but a lucky accident. There was not a wig in Paris large enough to harbor the great brain of the philosopher. A *perruquier* had brought him a wig on that memorable morning, and, after repeated efforts to put it on, dashed it angrily to the floor. "Is the wig too small?" asked the placid doctor. "No, monsieur; your head is too big!" roared the disgusted artist. So it came that Franklin went to court in the majesty of his own silver hair.

Franklin wore, when presented to the most brilliant court of Christendom, a full suit of plain black velvet, white ruffles at wrist and bosom, white-silk stockings, and silver buckles—the dress that the world is familiar with in Stuart's great revolutionary portraits. This was perhaps the first time, since heralds first went on embassies, that an envoy approached a sovereign in his own every-day garb.

Franklin was received in the dressing-room of the King. The monarch "had his hair, undressed, hanging down on his shoulders—no appearance of preparation to receive the Americans, no ceremony in doing it." There have not been, since embassies and alliances and wars were invented, many more important interviews than this, and a man must have the soul of a milliner if he thinks that the simplicity of this international greeting detracts anything from its dignity. For my part, I am pleased to think of this fine tableau of the perfect Pallas birth of American diplomacy displayed in the strong light of that historic day: the contrasted figures of the good, weak Louis and the great, wise Benjamin, greeting so simply, where the Republican paid conventional homage to the King, but where in reality the dying Past stood in the large presence of the great free Future.

Franklin became the fashion of the season. For the court itself dabbled a little in liberal ideas. So powerful was the vast impulse of free thought that then influenced the mind of France,—that susceptible French mind that always answers like the wind-harp to the breath of every true human aspiration,—that even the highest classes had caught the infection of liberalism. They handled the momentous words Liberty and Human Rights in their dainty way, as if they were only a new game for their amusement, not knowing what was to them the terrible import of those words. It became very much the accepted thing at court to rave about Franklin. The young and lovely Queen, Marie Antoinette, was most winning and gracious toward him. The languid courtiers crammed natural science to talk with him. The small wits who knew a little Greek called him Solon and Aristides and Phocion. It is sad to think of the utter unconsciousness of these amiable aristocrats. They never dreamed that this man Franklin was a portent and a prophet of ruin to them. He was incarnate Democracy, and they petted him! They never imagined that in showering their good-natured homage upon this austere republican they were sowing the wind which would ripen in an awful harvest of whirlwinds. Later, when the whirlwinds had hardly got beyond the frisky stage of their development, the Queen lamented bitterly the folly of these ovations to the great democrat. There was one sagacious head that was wisely shaken over these indiscretions while they lasted. Joseph II, Emperor of Austria, brother to the Queen, who was in Paris on his travels, and who was as much of a democrat himself as an emperor can be, when his sister rebuked his coolness on the American question, replied, "Madam, the trade I live by is that of a royalist."

Court incense could not turn the philosophic head any more than the loud acclaim of the people. When Franklin found himself the honored guest of royalty, his thoughts reverted to those far-away days of boyhood when his father used to quote to him, in the old candle-shop at Boston, the words of the wise man, "Seest thou a man diligent in his business? he shall stand before kings." The old sage heard the echo of that paternal voice resounding over half a century, and a new and strange light, as of prophecy fulfilled, illumined the immortal words. Surely no man ever lived more diligent in his business. Surely no man ever stood, with more of the innate dignity of upright manhood, before kings.

It was in this year of 1778 that Voltaire returned to Paris after an exile of thirty-seven years. It was like a visit to posterity. The France he had left existed no more. A new France, with a people and a public opinion, had come into the world, as bright, as critical, as aspiring as his own turbulent youth had been. The old man coming from the tranquil shades of Ferney, where he had dwelt for many years, still as his shadow, was dazed and bewildered by this fresh and vivid life, by this quick intellectual movement, this fervid homage of an intelligent people who had been born since he was young. He had lived so long that he had gained the unquestioning reverence due to the consecrated past. He breathed the sweet but deadly incense of posthumous fame. He was smothered under immortelles.

But before his frail life went out in the gale of popular adoration, he and Franklin met several times. At the first interview he laid his shadowy hands upon the head of Franklin's grandson and blessed him in the name of God and liberty. They met again on the platform of the French Academy. The crowd caught sight of the two patriarchs and clamorously roared that they should embrace, "*à la française.*" The two venerable men rose, approached, and kissed each other, to the wild delight of the entire vast assembly.

Rarely has a stranger contrast been seen in the world than when these two great geniuses clasped hands and kissed before that shouting people. They were both old men. But Voltaire belonged to a world that was passing away, and Franklin to a world just coming into being. Voltaire stood in the evening of his days, weary with conflict, glad of the coming rest, his work all behind him, forever. Born in the foulest days of monarchy, his alert and vivid intelligence had gone forth like the raven from the ark and had flown over the whole wide waste of earth and had found no green or healthful thing in church, or state, or sòciety. Everywhere unpitied suffering and unpunished crime, the cry of the desolate going up forever unheard. Whatever was, was wrong, and he armed his spirit for indiscriminate war. The work of his marvelously laborious life was therefore almost purely destructive. The ruins of the systems he had helped demolish were his only monument. To what better destinies was Franklin born! He came to the light among the stern, God-fearing Puritans. He grew up in a society whose virtues, say what you will, are as yet unequaled in history, and whose faults were those of earnest men. In dewy freshness and freedom as of the primeval morning, he and his great coadjutors began their beneficent work. They had nothing to destroy. Their godlike mission was to create. A struggle with outside resistance, and the mighty work was accomplished. Each effort of Franklin's life for the advancement of freedom and science had been founded on faith in God, from which springs belief in the innate goodness of man, and perfection of nature. God is good. His works are good. Doing good is doing his will, and is best. So, as he saw the shadows of the coming night grow long about his path, he could hope that, though he might pass away, his work would never perish. The torch he had lighted would pass from hand to hand down the ages. His labor would not be in vain as long as the lightning lived in the cloud or the thought of freedom in the mind of man.

This is the lesson we draw from this strange greeting of Franklin and Voltaire: to teach is better than to deny, to love and trust is wiser than to hate and doubt, to create is nobler than to destroy.

I have spared you many details of the diplomatic work of Franklin in these eventful years. You care only for results, and those you all know. Franklin, by the mere force of his personal character, obtained such influence with the French government that he rarely asked for anything that was not readily granted. He obtained from France the fleet of De Grasse and the army of Rochambeau. But, what was of vastly more importance, he obtained those timely grants of money from Versailles that saved us and helped "to bleed the French monarchy to death." And he kept the hands of the government from the heroic Paul Jones, and enabled him to inaugurate our naval history with a burst of glory amid which his dandy figure already stands half mythical in the light of his apparently impossible exploits. And finally he lent his masterly hand to the framing of the Treaty of Paris, by which drums were silenced and flags furled over the globe, and the United States took "the place among the nations of the earth to which the laws of nature and of nature's God entitled them."

His work abroad was over, and he begged to be permitted to return to the land he had so nobly served. But it was only in the spring of 1785 that Congress passed their resolution allowing the Hon. B. Franklin, Esq., to return to America and appointing the Hon. Thomas Jefferson, Esq., in his stead.

Franklin's journey from Paris to the sea-shore was one long festival. At the considerable towns which he passed the authorities received him with public honors and the great nobles disputed the privilege of entertaining him at their châteaux. It was not a republican demonstration. The old régime honored itself in its last days in nothing more than in its cordial appreciation of this artisan-philosopher.

This may have been one reason why Franklin, one of the most sagacious observers that ever lived, had apparently no clear perception of the tremendous change that was imminent in France. He heard in the court circles dilettante ideas of liberty discussed. The King was trying to redress in his inefficient way the deep-rooted wrongs of ages. There was a kind of false philanthropy in fashion. There was a specious show of revival of trade and commerce. There *were* two men at court—an old and a young man—who represented the new time, the vast and earnest future, but Franklin never seemed to recognize the significance of their attitude. For one of these men was himself and the other was Lafayette. He had returned from America matured by varied experience, educated by intercourse with the immortal rebels, perfectly attuned to the strange and swelling music of the age. He stood alone, calm and severe amid the gay crowd of courtiers, a chivalrous stoic among the amiable epicures of the decadence, at once a protest and a prophecy. While Franklin lived in Paris the personages of the dreadful scenes of '93 were scattered quietly over France, waiting for destiny to give their cue. Mirabeau he often entertained at Passy, for the wild young rake always loved letters and felt at home with philosophers. Danton was a broad-shouldered, briefless barrister, unknown out of the Latin Quarter. Robespierre was copying briefs at Arras, a dreamy enthusiast who fainted at the sight of blood. Marat came to Franklin one day, looking dirty and disreputable, with the smell of the Count d'Artois's stables about him, and with a scheme to destroy the British with elementary fire; and Charlotte Corday was a sweet little girl, the light of a quiet household in Normandy. And down in an Italian island, wearing out the seat of his trousers on a Corsican school-bench, was a moody, olive-complexioned boy named Buonaparte, who was to inspire the superb free France with so blind and mysterious a passion that she would follow him with unflinching adoration through slaughter and outrage to the gates of ruin.

All unconscious of these vivid colors scattered as yet unrecognizable in the loom of fate, Franklin sailed home to receive a welcome full of love and reverence, to be seized after scanty repose and put again in harness, to coöperate greatly in framing the Constitution—"work not unworthy men who strove with gods." Two of the last incidents of his life are lovingly remembered. It was he who introduced the motion in the Constitutional

Convention to open their meetings with prayer. His last Public act was to indite from his death-bed, as president of the Society for the Abolition of Slavery, a noble and touching appeal "for those unhappy men who, amidst the general joy of surrounding freemen, are groaning in servile subjection," in which the warm heart of the aged philanthropist seems united to the unerring conscience of the glorified saint. It is fitting that this beneficent and symmetrical life should be closed with this large utterance of humanity. Washington, Franklin, and Jefferson, in their mature age, scorning the dictates of a vulgar prudence, deliberately put on record their detestation of this growing crime. They at least believed in the words which make the Declaration immortal: "All men are created equal." I am glad to remember, too, that Lincoln, not many days before he went to join the august assembly of just men made perfect, said to me, "A man who denies to other men equality of rights is hardly worthy of freedom; but I would give *even to him* all the rights which I claim for myself." A plain phrase, but all the law and the prophets is in it.

FRANKLIN IN FRANCE

Franklin died in the night of the 17th of April, 1790. It is related that his last glance fell upon a picture of Christ on the cross.

It was the first great sorrow of the young nation. The people mourned for him. Madison made a speech of five minutes, and Congress wore mourning for a month—extraordinary honors in those days, from which we have somewhat worn the gloss since then.

The news reached France in June. The titanic games had begun. The mighty throes by which a nation was born were darting through the convulsed frame of society. The unchained Revolution, on which many had built absurd and fantastic hopes, was nearing that stage where many sank into equally absurd and fantastic despairs. Mirabeau was then the rugged and sparkling crest of the topmost wave. It was his clarion voice that announced to the National Assembly the death of the statesman and philosopher of two worlds, and sank into the wailing notes of a dirge as he recounted his virtues and glory. The delicate and sympathetic heart of France responded in a demonstration unique in the world's history. The Assembly and the nation turned for a time from their stupendous work to pay due honors to this alien tradesman. The hurricane stopped short in mid-career to waft a breath of tender regret to the grave of a citizen, growing green in the dewy hush of sunset a thousand leagues away.

OMAR KHAYYÁM

ADDRESS DELIVERED AT THE DINNER OF THE OMAR KHAYYÁM CLUB, LONDON, DECEMBER 8th, 1897. MR. HAY WAS THE GUEST OF THE CLUB.

OMAR KHAYYÁM

I CANNOT sufficiently thank you for the high and unmerited honor you have done me to-night. I feel keenly that on such an occasion, with such company, my place is below the salt; but as you kindly invited me, it was not in human nature for me to refuse.

Although in knowledge and comprehension of the two great poets whom you are met to commemorate I am the least among you, there is no one who regards them with greater admiration, or reads them with more enjoyment, than myself. I can never forget my emotions when I first saw FitzGerald's translations of the Quatrains. Keats, in his sublime ode on Chapman's Homer, has described the sensation once for all:

> Then felt I like some watcher of the skies
> When a new planet swims into his ken.

The exquisite beauty, the faultless form, the singular grace of those amazing stanzas were not more wonderful than the depth and breadth of their profound philosophy, their knowledge of life, their dauntless courage, their serene facing of the ultimate problems of life and of death. Of course the doubt did not spare me, which has assailed many as ignorant as I was of the literature of the East, whether it was the poet or his translator to whom was due this splendid result. Was it, in fact, a reproduction of an antique song, or a mystification of a great modern, careless of fame and scornful of his time? Could it be possible that in the eleventh century, so far away as Khorassan, so accomplished a man of letters lived, with such distinction, such breadth, such insight, such calm disillusion, such cheerful and jocund despair? Was this Weltschmerz, which we thought a malady of our day, endemic in Persia in 1100? My doubt only lasted till I came upon a literal translation of the Rubáiyát, and I saw that not the least remarkable quality of FitzGerald's poem was its fidelity to the original. In short, Omar was a FitzGerald before the letter, or FitzGerald was a reincarnation of Omar.

It is not to the disadvantage of the later poet that he followed so closely in the footsteps of the earlier. A man of extraordinary genius had appeared in the world; had sung a song of incomparable beauty and power in an environment no longer worthy of him, in a language of narrow range; for many generations the song was virtually lost; then by a miracle of creation, a poet, twin-brother in the spirit to the first, was born, who took up the forgotten poem and sang it anew with all its original melody and force, and with all the accumulated refinement of ages of art. It seems to me idle to ask which was the greater master; each seems greater than his work. The song is like an instrument of precious workmanship and marvelous tone, which is worthless in common hands, but when it falls, at long intervals, into the hands of the supreme master, it yields a melody of transcendent enchantment to all that have ears to hear.

If we look at the sphere of influence of the two poets, there is no longer any comparison. Omar sang to a half-barbarous province; FitzGerald to the world. Wherever the English speech is spoken or read, the Rubáiyát have taken their place as a classic. There is not a hill-post in India, nor a village in England, where there is not a coterie to whom Omar Khayyám is a familiar friend and a bond of union. In America he has an equal following, in many regions and conditions. In the Eastern States his adepts form an esoteric set; the beautiful volume of drawings by Mr. Vedder is a center of delight and suggestion wherever it exists. In the cities of the West you will find the Quatrains one of the most thoroughly read books in every club library. I heard them quoted once in one of the most lonely and desolate spots of the high Rockies. We had been camping on the Great Divide, our "roof of the world," where in the space of a few feet you may see two springs, one sending its waters to the Polar solitudes, the other to the eternal Carib summer. One morning at sunrise, as we were breaking camp, I was startled to hear one of our party, a frontiersman born, intoning these words of somber majesty:

'T is but a tent where takes his one day's rest
A Sultán to the realm of death addrest;

The Sultán rises, and the dark Ferrásh
Strikes and prepares it for another guest.

I thought that sublime setting of primeval forest and frowning cañon was worthy of the lines; I am sure the dewless, crystalline air never vibrated to strains of more solemn music.

Certainly, our poet can never be numbered among the great popular writers of all time. He has told no story; he has never unpacked his heart in public; he has never thrown the reins on the neck of the winged horse, and let his imagination carry him where it listed. "Oh! the crowd must have emphatic warrant," as Browning sang. Its suffrages are not for the cool, collected observer, whose eyes no glitter can dazzle, no mist suffuse. The many cannot but resent that air of lofty intelligence, that pale and subtle smile. But he will hold a place forever among that limited number who, like Lucretius and Epicurus,—without rage or defiance, even without unbecoming mirth,—look deep into the tangled mysteries of things; refuse credence to the absurd, and allegiance to arrogant authority; sufficiently conscious of fallibility to be tolerant of all opinions; with a faith too wide for doctrine and a benevolence untrammeled by creed, too wise to be wholly poets, and yet too surely poets to be implacably wise.

SIR WALTER SCOTT

ADDRESS AT UNVEILING OF BUST, WESTMINSTER ABBEY, MAY 21st, 1897.

SIR WALTER SCOTT

A CLEVER French author made a book some years ago called "The Forty-first Armchair." It consists of brief biographies of the most famous writers of France, none of whom had been members of the Academy. The astonishment of a stranger who is told that neither Molière nor Balzac was ever embraced among the "Forty Immortals" is very like that which has often affected the tourist who, searching among the illustrious names and faces which make this Abbey glorious, has asked in vain for the author of "Waverley."

It is not that he has ever been forgotten or neglected. His lines have gone out through all the earth, and his words to the end of the world. No face in modern history, if we may except the magisterial profile of Napoleon, is so well known as the winning, irregular features, dominated by the towering brow, of the

"Squire of Abbotsford." It is rather the world-wide extent of his fame that has seemed hitherto to make it unnecessary that his visible image should be shrined here among England's writers. His spirit is everywhere; he is revered wherever the English speech has traveled, and translations have given some glimpses of his brightness through the veil of many alien tongues; but the vastness of his name is no just reason why it may not have a local habitation also. It is therefore most fitting that his bust should be placed to-day among those of his mighty peers, in this great Pantheon of immortal Englishmen.

In this most significant and interesting ceremony I should have no excuse for appearing, except as representing for the time being a large section of Walter Scott's immense constituency. I doubt if anywhere his writings have had a more loving welcome than in America. The books a boy reads are those most ardently admired and the longest remembered; and America reveled in Scott when the country was young. I have heard from my father, a pioneer of Kentucky, that in the early days of this century men would saddle their horses and ride from all the neighboring counties to the principal post-town of the region when a new novel by the author of "Waverley" was expected. All over our straggling states and territories—in the East, where a civilization of slender resources but boundless hopes was building; in the West, where the stern conflict was going on of the pioneer subduing the continent—the books most read were those poems of magic and of sentiment, those tales of bygone chivalry and romance, which Walter Scott was pouring forth upon the world with a rich facility, a sort of joyous fecundity like that of Nature in her most genial moods. He had no clique of readers, no illuminated sect of admirers, to bewilder criticism by excess of its own subtlety. In a community engaged in the strenuous struggle for empire, whose dreams, careless of the past, were turned in the clear, broad light of a nation's morning to a future of unlimited grandeur and power, there was none too sophisticated to appreciate, none too lowly to enjoy those marvelous pictures of a time gone forever by, pleasing and stimulating to a starved fancy in the softened light of memory and art, though the times themselves were unlamented by a people and an age whose faces were set toward a far-different future.

Through all these important formative days of the Republic, Scott was the favorite author of Americans, and, while his writings may not be said to have had any special weight in our material and political development, yet their influence was enormous upon the taste and the sentiments of a people peculiarly sensitive to such influences from the very circumstances of their environment. The romances of courts and castles were specially appreciated in the woods and prairies of the frontier, where a pure democracy reigned. The poems and novels of Scott, saturated with the glamor of legend and tradition, were greedily devoured by a people without perspective, conscious that they themselves were ancestors of a redoubtable line, whose battle was with the passing hour, whose glories were all in the days to come.

Since the time of Scott we have seen many fashions in fiction come and go; each generation naturally seeks a different expression of its experience and its ideals, but the author of "Waverley," amid all vicissitudes of changing modes, has kept his preëminence in two hemispheres as the master of imaginative narration. Even those of us who make no pretensions to the critical faculty may see the twofold reason of this enduring masterhood. Both mentally and morally Scott was one of the greatest writers that ever lived. His mere memory, his power of acquiring and retaining serviceable facts, was almost inconceivable to ordinary men, and his constructive imagination was nothing short of prodigious. The lochs and hills of Scotland swarm with the imaginary phantoms with which he has peopled them for all time; the historical personages of past centuries are jostled in our memories by the characters he has created, more vivid in vitality and color than the real soldiers and lovers with whom he has cast their lives.

But probably the morality of Scott appeals more strongly to the many than even his enormous mental powers. His ideals are lofty and pure; his heroes are brave and strong, not exempt from human infirmities, but always devoted to ends more or less noble. His heroines, whom he frankly asks you to admire, are beautiful and true. They walk in womanly dignity through his pages, whether garbed as peasants or as princesses, with honest brows uplifted, with eyes gentle but fearless, pure in heart and delicate in speech; valor, purity and loyalty—these are the essential and undying elements of the charm with which this great magician has soothed and lulled the weariness of the world through three tormented generations. For this he has received the uncritical, ungrudging love of grateful millions.

His magic still has power to charm all wholesome and candid souls. Although so many years have passed since his great heart broke in the valiant struggle against evil fortune, his poems and his tales are read with undiminished interest and perennial pleasure. He loved with a simple, straightforward affection man and nature, his country and his kind; he has his reward in a fame forever fresh and unhackneyed. The poet who as an infant clapped his hands and cried "Bonnie!" to the thunderstorm, and whose dying senses were delighted by the farewell whisper of the Tweed rippling over its pebbles, is quoted in every aspect of sun and shadow that varies the face of Scotland. The man who blew so clear a clarion of patriotism lives forever in the speech of those who seek a line to describe the love of country. The robust, athletic spirit of his tales of old, the loyal quarrels, the instructive loves, the stanch devotion of the uncomplicated creations of his inexhaustible fancy—all these have their special message and attraction for the minds of our day, fatigued with problems, with doubts and futile questionings. His work is a clear, high voice, from a simpler age than ours, breathing a song of lofty and unclouded purpose, of sincere and powerful passion, to which the world, however weary and preoccupied, must needs still listen and attend.

SPEECHES BEFORE THE AMERICAN SOCIETY IN LONDON

SPEECHES BEFORE THE AMERICAN SOCIETY IN LONDON

FAREWELL BANQUET GIVEN TO MR. AND MRS. BAYARD, MAY 7th, 1897.

I HAVE no suitable words to express my appreciation of the most kind and flattering language of the Lord Chief Justice, and of the amiability with which you have received the mention of my name. There is no time to develop the thought that the Lord Chief Justice has expressed of the duties of an ambassador. I can only say that I adopt his words in their entirety, and that the dearest wish of my heart is that the happy relations now subsisting between the two great nations may be not only continued, but, if possible, drawn still closer during the time that I shall hold the office of ambassador. When your chairman kindly invited me to come here this evening, and Mr. Bayard added the sanction of his own friendly request, I could not deny myself the opportunity of passing so delightful an evening in your company, but I stipulated that I was to come here not in an official capacity, but as an American, temporarily resident in London, to add the tribute of my regard to your distinguished guest. You will, therefore, not expect me to abuse your kindness by taking any extended part in the evening's proceedings; but I must express the pleasure I feel at being here.

Mr. Bayard and I—if I may couple great things with small—have been cordially opposed to each other all our lives, and I doubt not we are still opposed in almost every matter of public moment upon which men of good will may differ; but I have always been happy and proud of his personal friendship. I have always appreciated the dignity, the charm, and the grace of his character, and I have shared with all his friends the pleasure they took in tne unexampled affection and popularity which he has conquered in England. There are successes which provoke neither envy nor emulation. It would be most injudicious for any immediate successor of Mr. Bayard to attempt to rival his brilliant career, or to try to replace him in the regard of the British people. Such an attempt could end in nothing but disaster. None but Ulysses himself could bend the bow of Ulysses. I could only rival Mr. Bayard in singleness of purpose to preserve intact the most friendly relations between the United States and England. He will always be remembered as our first Ambassador, and as much more than that. He has gained the affectionate esteem, not only of the Government and the governing classes, but of the masses of the population in these islands. Since the great French Revolution, which brought the people forward as the principal factor of sovereignty, it has been a fashion of French Kings and Emperors to call themselves Emperors and Kings, not of France, but of the French. In like manner it would not be inappropriate to speak of Mr. Bayard, not so much as Ambassador to England, as Ambassador to the English. I join you heartily in wishing him and his family God-speed, a prosperous voyage, and many years of health and happiness at home.

INDEPENDENCE DAY BANQUET,
MONDAY, JULY 5TH, 1897.

I AM glad to be here on this slightly dislocated Independence Day. The Fourth of July is a necessary and wholesome antidote to our American vice of modesty. There was a good deal of discussion and some agitation among the newspapers of America some years ago—and there was a good deal less of public interest in the question—as to what flower could be most properly adopted as our national emblem. I have forgotten how the discussion was decided. It probably never was decided at all. The great advantage of newspaper discussions is that they do not need to be decided. I have no doubt as to what the decision ought to have been. The national American flower ought to be the violet—the emblem of modesty and self-effacement. I have never been at a Fourth of July meeting of Americans without being impressed that this quality of modesty might be pushed too far. It would be most unwise to attempt to change this shrinking and shy character of the American people into anything that savored of arrogance and self-assertion, but if there is one day in the year on which we might be justified in letting the eagle scream a little, it is this day—or the day before.

Dr. Potter has praised me and Mr. Reid, but not a word had been said in praise of Uncle Sam; and yet I think we have a right on a day like this to blow our own trumpet a little, or —to use the words of Walt Whitman—to sound our barbaric yawp over the roofs of the world. If this were the time for criticism, we might find many little things to censure, but let us think how many things we have to rejoice over. There is no country in the world, I believe, where there is more freedom, more enterprise, more public and private morality, than in America. The great historian, Mr. Henry Adams, in his admirable history of the earlier administrations, says there are two characteristics of this new people and this new nation which are clear: we are sure to be intelligent, and we are sure to be good-natured. Every year that has passed of our national existence had proved that assertion. We have had few quarrels. When we have been forced to fight, we have fought without much malice, and although we have sometimes, perhaps, been less soft-spoken than we might have been, yet we have practised with reasonable consistency, for more than a hundred years, the old-fashioned doctrine of "Peace on earth, good will towards men." We desire peace and amity with the whole world. I need not say how sincerely we desire it with that great people whose guests we are, and to whom we are bound by so many ties. The affection that goes out from our hearts to England simply proves that the blood in our veins is true to the original spring. The unity with England in this year of Jubilee shows how near together the two countries are in spirit, though sundered by so many leagues of the "unsociable sea." We are absolutely at one in our appreciation of the great and good Sovereign who, in her long and happy reign, has shown how compatible are the highest qualities of a monarch with the purest virtues of private life. Such a reign, however indefinitely prolonged, can never be too long for the happiness of her people.

THANKSGIVING DAY BANQUET,
NOVEMBER 25TH, 1897.

THE great body of the peoples of England and of the United States are friends. There is, of course, no doubt of that—any other relation would be madness. If there is one class of men in either country who more than all others appreciate that fact, and the necessity of it, it is the great lawyers of America and the great lawyers of Great Britain. The reason for this is not far to seek. It is to be found in that intense respect and reverence for order, liberty, and law which is so profound a sentiment in both countries. Strong as that sentiment is in England, it is naturally not less strong in America, where we feel ourselves, and are grateful to acknowledge, that we are the fortunate heirs of English liberty and English law. With respect to the national festival of thanksgiving, it injures no one. There can never be too much gratitude in the world; and seventy millions of voices praising God together will not justify the adding of a single ironclad to any navy in the world.

INDEPENDENCE DAY BANQUET, JULY 4TH, 1898.

I SHOULD be much to be commiserated if I were expected to say anything new and original in proposing the toast which has been confided to me. A hundred and twenty-one celebrations like this have exhausted the resources of eulogy; we must be content to repeat the phrases of our fathers. But there are some words which never pall upon the ear; there are songs which have gained in melody for centuries; and the praise of this day will not seem stale to any audience of Americans until the nation begins to falter and halt in its triumphant march of progress. Thank Heaven! it is beyond the power of prophecy to foretell that day of evil omen to the world.

To how many people to-day the thought must have occurred—how fortune seems to favor this day of all days in the year; how history seems determined to regild it from time to time, consecrating it anew to glory and use. First in Philadelphia in 1776; then in 1863 a double splendor lighted upon it, illuminating a continent from Vicksburg to Gettysburg; and now the world is spanned with its brilliancy from Santiago to Manila, from the Antilles to the Antipodes.

This year all the omens are with us. The presence at this board of so many of the most eminent representatives of English life seems like a visible sign and symbol of the new amity, too long delayed, between the two great branches of the English-speaking people. For many reasons this will be a memorable year; for none more than for the lucid recognition, by the British and American communities alike, of the fact that, reversing the text, the ways of pleasantness between them are the ways of wisdom, and that variance is mere folly and madness. We are glad to think that this is no passing emotion, born of a troubled hour; it has been growing through many quiet years. I am reminded of a little parable. A friend of mine, known and honored by all of you, who had taken a castle in Scotland, wanted to display the British and American flags from its topmost tower. But not wishing to give either precedence over the other, he had the two flags sewed together, so that one side displayed the Stars and Stripes and the other the meteor flag of England. The combination was rather —I will not say heavy, but weighty, and in the still days of midsummer it drooped upon the staff. But when a breeze came the twin flags unfolded the splendor of their colors, and when a gale blew they stood stiffly out to the air, proclaiming their attachment to every quarter of the sky. So my friend drew the moral which

I see you recognize before I utter it. The attachment was formed long ago, but it needed rough weather to show it to the world.

Now that the day of clear and cordial understanding has come which so many of us have long desired and waited for, may we not hope it is to last for ever? It threatens no one; it injures no one; its ends are altogether peaceful and beneficent. We shall still compete with each other and the rest of the world, but the competition will be in the arts and the works of civilization, and all the people of good-will on the face of the earth will profit by it.

Whenever I speak on this auspicious day I have to brace myself against the temptations of saying too much. We do not want to be too robustious and forthputting, especially in the presence of these our good friends who have been so kind as to share our modest revels. But let us never forget, as we think we have a right to remember, that this day has been a day of good augury to mankind. When all allowances are made, all censures duly weighed, when we have confessed that there are many things among us which need to be mended or ended, the fact remains that the great experiment our forefathers set on foot has resulted in enormous good, not only to ourselves, but to the world. Even the mighty motherland is the richer by the consequences of that sharp wrench by which we tore ourselves free. We have been preaching for a hundred years, not always consistently, not always in the best taste or with purest accent, a gospel, the tendency of which is for ever towards the light, and the result of which has been the breaking of fetters, the freeing of those who sat in darkness, the lifting of cruel burdens from the shoulders of the poor. It is sometimes said that we exalt this mass to the detriment of the individual—but the system which in our earliest years gave us a Washington and in our later years a Lincoln, is not likely to condemn the race to monotonous sterility and decay. There are those who think that in our keen pursuit of material gain we may have lost our pristine loyalty and devotion. But I am old enough to have seen, at an insult to the flag, a million peace-loving men rushing to arms and crowding "the road of death as to a festival."

I am not permitted to discuss the events of

the hour, but I make bold to predict that at any time of need the nation will be found as prompt and efficient in war, as clement and generous in victory, as in those days which a great English poet sang about in these splendid lines:

> Lo! how fair from afar!
> Blameless in victory stands
> Thy mighty daughter, for years
> Who trod the winepress of war,
> Shines with immaculate hands;
> Slays not a foe, neither fears—
> Stains not peace with a scar.

The men of our race have never proved themselves unworthy of good fortune in the hour of success. The nation which ended a vast rebellion without an execution or a bill of attainder may be trusted always to be moderate and magnanimous in victory. I believe that when the bitterness of our present troubles shall have passed away, both parties will be found to have profited by the issue—the one by the assertion of a principle which will conduce to the peace of the world, and the other by the removal of burdens and responsibilities which had grown too heavy to be borne.

A PARTNERSHIP IN BENEFICENCE

SPEECH AT EASTER BANQUET, MANSION HOUSE, LONDON, APRIL 21st, 1898, IN RESPONSE TO THE LORD MAYOR'S TOAST TO THE AMBASSADORS AND FOREIGN MINISTERS PRESENT ON THIS OCCASION

A PARTNERSHIP IN BENEFICENCE

I AM honored in having the privilege of thanking you, on behalf of all my colleagues as well as myself, and the countries which we represent, for the cordiality with which this toast has been proposed and the kindness with which it has been received. In this place, the civic heart of London, the home of a traditional and princely hospitality, whence from time immemorial the only challenge that has gone forth has been one inviting the world to that wholesome competition in civilizing arts which benefits all parties to it, we cannot but accept this courtesy in the spirit in which it is tendered, and in return wish success and prosperity to England and to British trade and commerce, in the full assurance that all the nations of the world will profit more or less directly by every extension of British commerce and the enterprise and enlightenment that go with it hand-in-hand.

Perhaps I may be pardoned if I say a word about my own country. Knitted as we are to the people of Great Britain by a thousand ties, of origin, of language, and of kindred pursuits, it is inevitable that from time to time we should have occasions of discussion and even of difference. We hear sometimes that we are thought to be somewhat eager and pertinacious in the pursuit of our own interests. If that is so, I can say, I hope with no impertinence, and in a spirit rather of pride than of contrition, that it merely goes to show of what stock we are. But this truth is unquestionable—that for now nearly three generations of men there has been peace between us and friendly regard, a peace growing more solid and durable as years go by, and a friendship that I am sure the vast majority of both peoples hope and trust is to be eternal. The reasons of a good understanding between us lie deeper than any considerations of mere expediency. All of us who think cannot but see that there is a sanction like that of religion which binds us to a sort of partnership in the beneficent work of the world. Whether we will it or not, we are associated in that work by the very nature of things, and no man and no group of men can prevent it. We are bound by a tie which we did not forge and which we cannot break; we are joint ministers of the same sacred mission of liberty and progress, charged with duties which we cannot evade by the imposition of irresistible hands.

It may be trite and even tedious for me to refer again at this distance of time to the mighty pageant of last June, but I may ask leave to recall one incident of the naval review, which will long be remembered by those who saw it. On the evening of that memorable day, when all the ships lay enshrouded in darkness, the commander of the *Brooklyn* ran up the British and American colors, and then at a given signal turned upon those two kindred flags the brilliant rays of her searchlights. In that high illumination shrined in clear radiance far above the obscurity that hid the engines of destruction and preparations for war, those friendly banners fluttered, proclaiming to the navies of the world their message of good will. The beauty of the scene lasted but a moment; it passed away with much of the splendor and magnificence that adorned the historic day; but may we not hope that the lesson and the inspiration of that spectacle may last as long as those banners shall float over the seven seas, carrying always in their shadow freedom and civilization?

SPEECH AT THE ANNUAL DINNER OF THE ROYAL SOCIETY

UNDER THE PRESIDENCY OF LORD LISTER, NOVEMBER 30th, 1897

SPEECH AT THE ANNUAL DINNER OF THE ROYAL SOCIETY

I MIGHT begin by pleading the brevity of the notice which has been given me of the undeserved honor which lay in wait for me on entering these hospitable walls. But as I should have been almost equally unprepared, no matter what notice I might have received, I need not dwell upon this detail.

I never have been able, I never shall be, to speak adequately in this place, or to such a company. If I have one qualification, I have only one, to appear before you. As the commission I hold is the sole reason for my being invited here, so the only personal aptitude I possess, for raising my voice among you, is the feeling that I am in harmony with those sentiments of world-wide concord and amity which form the dominant note of all that is ever said when men of science or men of learning meet on either shore of the Atlantic.

I regret I have not even the smattering of science which would enable me to put on the appearance of saying anything instructive or amusing. The only reason why I do not stand entirely mute is that I am unwilling by silence to seem insensible to the great compliment paid me in assigning me to this honorable duty.

It is in bodies of men like this, on both sides of the sea, in institutions like your own and similar ones of more recent date and narrower resources in America, that there exists one of the strongest bonds of union among the two great branches of our race. They are held together by the common love and pursuit of universal truth, by devotion to the best interests of mankind, by a kindred passion for light and progress. These are among the strongest incentives to harmonious action known among men. In your pursuits everything unites, nothing divides. The results of science are all gain and no loss.

The triumphs of war are bought by tears and anguish on both sides; the successes of diplomacy and of trade are often attended by the discomfiture of one of the parties; but the whole world is brightened and made more agreeable by the achievements of Morse or Faraday; the genius of Lister and of Morton diminishes beyond computation the whole vast sum of human suffering; and every discovery or invention, on either side of the ocean, the product of the searching, self-denying scholars of our race—Edison or Lord Kelvin, Graham Bell or Bessemer, Darwin or Marsh — is at once thrown into the common stock of the world's intellectual riches, profiting every one and injuring none.

It is for this reason that I—though I have no other right to sit among scholars or men of science,—since the object of my mission here is to do what I can to draw closer the bonds that bind together the two Anglo-Saxon peoples,—it is for this reason that I am glad to come here and to offer my tribute of profound respect to these eminent men who, under the auspices of this venerable Society, are doing so much to hasten the coming of the day when misunderstandings and misconception shall fade away in the light of truth and widening knowledge, and universal peace "shall lie like a shaft of light across the lands, and like a line of beams athwart the sea."

SPEECH AT THE ANNUAL DINNER OF THE LITERARY FUND

UNDER THE PRESIDENCY OF THE DUKE OF DEVONSHIRE
MAY 17th, 1898

SPEECH AT THE ANNUAL DINNER OF THE LITERARY FUND

MY LORD DUKE, my Lords and Gentlemen: I have no words to express my gratitude for the courtesy with which Mr. Justice Madden has mentioned my name, and the extreme amiability with which you have received it. I had some hesitation in accepting the kind invitation of Lord Crewe to come to this dinner. My connection with Literature, I knew, had not been sufficiently distinguished to entitle me to any such invitation. But I remembered the principle on which a four-in-hand club was organized some years ago in America; there were eligible two classes of the community, those who drove four-in-hand, and those who would like to if they could. I felt that under some such category as the last I might ask to be admitted to the company of men of letters, and perhaps the fact that one is not to be ranked amongst the famous writers of the world makes him all the freer in speaking of the things of the spirit, as in doing so he is not magnifying his own office. Though, to do them justice, this consideration has not always kept the seers and the poets tongue-tied. Horace talks of having built for himself a monument more lasting than bronze. My old friend Walt Whitman delighted in speaking of himself as "one of the roughs, a Cosmos, a man no more modest than immodest." And an Egyptian poet, beside whom Horace and Whitman seem almost equally modern, has said in the dim days before Moses, "To all professions but one there is some objection; only the scribe is, without question, pre-eminent." And, after all, there are some subjects on which exaggeration is well-nigh impossible, and one of them is the masterful influence of the best Literature. The mightiest kings reign and die and are forgotten, or only their names remain; but great writers have a tenure of power unlimited by ages. I read with delight when I was a child the late Mr. Kinglake's "Eothen," and I have never forgotten the chapter in which he describes himself toiling over wretched roads to visit a ruined temple of the Paphian Venus. Why did he—why do all of us make these world-wide pilgrimages to temples and fanes which are nothing but crumbling stones and broken shards? The gods are gone; they can do nothing for us, whatever they once may have done, to cure life's fever and pain. They have lost the blessed power of illusion. We go, as Kinglake did, because of a verse of Virgil, a line of Homer, which has consecrated those shrines for ever. As you sail by the coast of Sicily it is most likely that you think not so much of the stirring events of history of which it has been the theatre, as of some verse, some phrase of Theocritus which has made it an enchanted land. The fascinations of Cleopatra live more surely in the lines of Shakespeare than in the sculpture and paintings on the massive walls of Denderah.

There is no term, no date to really great Literature. The Book of Job comes home to our hearts as though it were written yesterday. Even when the works of the master singers are gone and have perished from men's memory, their fame lives on for countless ages like the life of the spirit when the body is dust. We need no poems of Sappho to be sure that she was one of the greatest of poets. It must be confessed that it is only among the firstborn of genius that we may expect this immortal royalty. For the common run of us, we can adopt the sad sincerity of the remark of Mr. Howells, when, speaking about that pathetic complaint so common among young writers, of the oblivion which is to overtake them hereafter, he says, "We do not dream, in our innocence, of that shoreless sea of oblivion in which we welter all our lives." In such a company as this, I hesitate to hint at the mortality of literary fame. I might borrow a leaf from the book of a French clergyman who was preaching before Louis XV. He had been told that the king was not pleased at any reference to his latter end; but, carried away by the fervor of his discourse, he was so unlucky as to say, "Brethren, we must all die," then, remembering the august presence in which he stood, he added, "at least, most of us." I think I may go that far even here.

But whatever our rank in the hierarchy, whatever our span of existence, the glory of the writer, in which the highest as well as the lowest may share, is that in his art there is something which transcends the ordinary laws of demand and supply. The most considerable efforts of genius have been either ill-paid or not paid at all. The most eminent philosophers and historians, from the time of Aristotle and Thucydides down to our own days, have regarded very little, if at all, the material gain of their work. If there had been no such thing as money in the world, "Lycidas" and "In Memoriam" would have been written all the same. Keats and Shelley, had they been paupers or millionaires, would still have given forth those immortal notes, twin Memnons smitten by the morning light. The worst-paid poet in America produced the most exquisite lyrics to which our country has given birth. Edgar Poe received with pathetic gratitude the few dollars which were grudgingly doled out to him for those masterpieces of a melody so fine and magical that they seem like music heard in dreams. A new song by Burns would be worth how many guineas? But all the guineas in Threadneedle Street will not give us another. Unquestionably, the amount of the literary product is increased by just and proper compensation. The quantity of Literature produced can be augmented by money, but quality is beyond the power of gold.

We hear it sometimes said that the gods are vanished and that only the half-gods remain. It cannot be denied that on both sides of the Atlantic a great constellation of stars has left the heavens all at once. Perhaps we are to pass through an hour or two of dubious twilight, but even if this condition is admitted, this *Dichterdaemmerung,* we cannot forget that the twilight is a phase of the dawn as well as of the night. Literature can never perish from the earth, and English Literature, like the British Empire, can never be wholly swallowed up in darkness. Somewhere, always, in that immense expanse the sun will be shining. Even if your soil should lie fallow in the Metropolis for a time, at the ends of the earth there will be fecundity and bloom. Even if the tuneful choir should rest for a few bars in England—of which, I am bound to say, I see no sign whatever,—the English lark, though he spring from Canadian meadows or the Indian jungle, will still be heard singing at Heaven's gate. I do not speak of my own people, because I have no time to enumerate the young writers who, beyond the sea, are beginning to flame in the forehead of the morning sky. It is, therefore, with no spirit of pessimism, no looking backward with despair to the great departed who were my contemporaries, but forward, with the brightest hope, the fullest confidence, to the vast future, that I welcome, and give thanks for, the old and ever new toast of Literature.

SPEECH AT THE OPENING, BY MISS HELEN HAY, OF THE ROBERT BROWNING GARDEN

YORK STREET, WALWORTH, LONDON, JUNE 13th, 1898

SPEECH AT THE OPENING, BY MISS HELEN HAY, OF THE ROBERT BROWNING GARDEN

I AM sure you will not expect me to make a speech this evening. I came merely to pay my homage to the illustrious memory of Browning and my tribute of respect to the excellent work which is going on here in his name. It seems to me that nothing could be more appropriate; the name of Browning stands as a symbol of intellectual energy and moral earnestness and is most fittingly used in any effort to uplift and enlighten men. Especially is it an appropriate symbol in all attempts to benefit the people; for though he unquestionably belonged to the great aristocracy of genius and character, there never was a more uncompromising democrat in the essential, underlying principles of true democracy. To him all men were equal in the sight of God. He believed in equality of rights, equality of opportunity, equality in the individual sacredness of soul of every man and every woman. And the first of all rights—the right to the light—he always upheld and vindicated with all the power of his wonderful poetry and the example of his blameless life.

This is the spirit which breathes through all his work, beginning with the "veined humanity" of "Bells and Pomegranates,' developing in fullness and splendor through all the stately procession of his songs, to reach that noble climax of music and color and radiance which finally charmed and conquered the world in "Men and Women." From beginning to end, from youth through glorious manhood to serene old age, his lyre was always true to the one unfaltering tone, which taught the innate dignity of human nature,—its right always to learn, always to aspire.

We may be sure, therefore, that this most laudable effort to keep alight in this the most densely-populated region of London the torch of moral and intellectual culture is one of the things he would heartily have commended while living, and upon which his glorified spirit, if it were permitted to revisit the scenes of his earthly pilgrimage, would be certain to look with lofty and benignant approval.

I wish to say nothing more except to thank you from the bottom of my heart, on my own behalf and that of my daughter, for the most amiable and kindly way in which you have received us, and for the pleasure we have enjoyed in being with you this evening, and most of all for the kindly and cordial words of sympathy with our country which we have heard not only from the speakers but from this audience. You may be sure that no words of goodwill however strong, however enthusiastic, can be uttered in England that will not find instant and adequate response on the other side of the Atlantic. For myself, of whom you have spoken but too kindly, I can only say that a frank and warm friendship with England has been one of the passions of my life. The hope of it I have cherished ever since I knew anything, and I am glad that I have lived long enough to see the dawn of it upon the horizon.

INTERNATIONAL COPYRIGHT

LETTER TO THE POET LAUREATE

INTERNATIONAL COPYRIGHT

Department of State

Washington, May 23, 1899.

MY DEAR MR. AUSTIN: I owe you many apologies for my delay in answering your letter, of which I am ashamed to give the date. I think you would pardon me if you knew how my time has been occupied. Even now I shall not attempt to write a letter like yours. Long before it reached my hands it had been read with enjoyment wherever there are readers who care for good thoughts expressed in perfect English. I cannot vie with you in such a competition. Nor can I discuss the subject of copyright with any such authority as you possess. The laurel you bear makes you the dean of contemporary English literature. My place in the world of letters is too inconsiderable to give me any title to speak for

American authors, and the post I hold for the moment in the Government not only confers no power over legislation, but even restricts to some extent that liberty of criticism and suggestion which would be my right as a private citizen.

I am, however, as you assume, greatly interested in the subject of international copyright. I sympathized, and, to the extent of my ability, co-operated with the efforts of men more energetic and capable than myself to reform our objectionable copyright system and to have the present arrangement enacted into law. I think you do something less than justice to the law itself and to the Congress that enacted it. There were many interests opposed to it, and it required no little patience and care to bring together the different groups of opinion favorable to the principle involved. The law as passed was not what everybody wanted, but it was the only settlement within reach, and it was in itself, I venture to say, if not perfect in all its provisions, a most laudable and beneficent act. Its good effects have surpassed the expectations of its friends.

From inquiries I have recently made I am

led to believe that the operation of the law has not profited American publishers to anything like the extent they anticipated, and while it has certainly been an advantage to American authors, they have not been its chief beneficiaries. English writers have profited largely by the protection afforded them, and English publishers have reaped great advantage by establishing branch offices in this country, which have enabled them to handle their English business at inconsiderable expense and to extend their profitable operations here.

It is not in its application to pure literature alone that our law of copyright ought to be judged. In the department of art it affords absolutely perfect security to producers, all rights in paintings, etchings, drawings, sculpture and architectural plans being reserved by simple registry at a nominal fee. The same is true of musical works of all sorts. Recent legal decisions have taken the highest ground, following the purpose of the framers of the law, in affording to music the most liberal protection. Dramatic works also receive the most ample security. They are better protected, I am informed, than even in England.

It is in the matter of the manufacture of books alone that the complaint of the English author is founded, and I cannot but think that the hardships which are alleged to proceed from this source are somewhat exaggerated. The operation of the law has been in the main of enormous value to English authors, both in their financial returns and the spread of their fame and influence. In many cases the prices of literary work under the action of the law have more than doubled. The world of English letters was never so prosperous as now. The hardship of compelling the manufacture of English books in America has greatly decreased with the constantly diminishing cost of the work, and where a book impresses a publisher as worthy his attention the question of the outlay for printing is hardly regarded. Where such a book has not seemed of sufficient value to be reprinted here, the author has, of course, been free to import a foreign edition, but I am told there has not been an instance in which this has operated disadvantageously to a later edition of the work or to the author's next book.

The growth of respect for literary property

has always been proportionate to the familiarity with literary exchange, and since the passage of our law the security conferred upon many people formerly indifferent to the subject has created for the copyright law a body of new supporters. It is a great advantage to feel that no backward step will be taken, and the almost unanimous voice of American men of letters, including the entire league of American authors and not a few of our most prominent publishers, is in cordial sympathy with your own lofty and generous aspiration for the absolute freedom of literary exchange throughout the world.

I know you will pardon the inadequacy of this reply to your most gracious and magnanimous letter, and let me say in conclusion with what sincere cordiality I welcome and return your expressions of good will. Your genial words have found only sympathetic echoes throughout this country. We are, and from the nature of the case must always be, keen competitors in the work of the world, but, whatever details may intervene of political or commercial rivalry, the blood in our veins, the history in our memories, must always make us yoke-fellows in the weighty tasks laid upon us which make for civilization and for righteousness.

Believe me, my dear Mr. Austin, with happy memories of our last meeting, and pleasant anticipations of the next, faithfully yours,

JOHN HAY.

AMERICAN DIPLOMACY

SPEECH IN REPLY TO THE TOAST OF "OUR RECENT DIPLOMACY"
AT NEW YORK CHAMBER OF COMMERCE DINNER
NOVEMBER 19th, 1901

AMERICAN DIPLOMACY

I NEED not dwell upon the mournful and tragic event by virtue of which I am here. When the President lay stricken in Buffalo, though hope beat high in all our hearts that his life might be spared for future usefulness to his country, it was still recognized as improbable that he should be able to keep the engagement he had made to be with you to-night, and your committee did me the honor to ask me to come in his place. This I have sometimes done, in his lifetime, though always with diffidence and dread; but how much more am I daunted by the duty of appearing before you when that great man, loved and revered above all even while living, has put on the august halo of immortality! Who could worthily come into your presence as the shadow of that illustrious Shade?

Let me advert, but for a moment, to one aspect of our recent bereavement, which is especially interesting to those engaged, as you are, in relations whose scope is as wide as the world. Never, since history began, has there been an event which so immediately, and so deeply, touched the sensibilities of so vast a portion of the human race. The sun, which set over Lake Erie while the surgeons were still battling for the President's life, had not risen on the Atlantic before every capital of the civilized world was in mourning. And it was not from the centers of civilization alone that the voices of sorrow and sympathy reached us; they came as well from the utmost limits of the world, from the most remote islands of the sea; not only from the courts of Christendom, but from the temples of strange gods and the homes of exotic religions. Never before has the heart of the world throbbed with a sorrow so universal. Never before have the kingdoms of the earth paid such homage at the grave of a citizen. Something of this was naturally due to his great office—presiding, as he did, over the government of a nation holding in fee the certainty of illimitable greatness. But no ruler can acquire the instinctive regard and esteem of the world without possessing most unusual qualities of mind and character. This dead President of ours possessed them. He was strong; he was wise; he was gentle. With no external advantages beyond the mass of his fellow-citizens, he rose by sheer merit and will to the summit of distinction and power. With a growth as certain and gradual as that of an oak, he grew stronger and wiser with every year that he lived. Confronted continually with new and exacting situations, he was never unequal to them; his serenity was never clouded; he took the storm and the sunshine with the same cheery welcome; his vast influence expanded with his opportunities. Like that Divine Master whom he humbly and reverently served, he grew continually "in favor with God and man."

One simple reason why the millions of this country mourned him as if they had buried a brother, and why all the nations of the earth felt that his death was a loss to humanity at large, was that he loved his fellow-men. There were literally no bounds to his lavish good will. In political genius, in wisdom for government, in power of controlling men, he was one of the elect of the earth—there were few like him; but in sentiment and feeling he was the most perfect democrat I ever met. He never knew what it meant to regard another man as his inferior, or as his superior. Nothing human was alien to him. Even his death was in that sense significant. He was slain in the moment when with that delightful smile we knew so well—which seemed like the very sunshine of the spirit—he was stretching forth a generous hand to greet the lowest and meanest unit in that crowd of many thousands. He made no demagogical parade of his sympathy with the masses, but this sympathy was a part of his life. He knew no interest which was not theirs; their welfare was as dear to him as the blood in his own veins; and in spite of calumny and falsehood the people knew it, and they loved him in return.

Others will rise and labor and do good service to the Republic. We shall never lack good men when the emergency calls for them. Thank God! we do not lack them now. But it may well be doubted if in any century of the glorious future before us, there will ever appear two such sincere, high-minded, self-respecting lovers of the people as the last fifty years have shown us in Abraham Lincoln and William McKinley.

But the world must go on, though the greatest and best beloved fall by the way. I dare to come to you, because you have asked me, and he would have wished it, for he held that our personal feelings should never be considered when they conflicted with a public duty. And if I fall immeasurably below the standard to which he has accustomed you, the very comparisons you draw will be a tribute to his memory.

I am asked to say something about our diplomacy. You want from me nothing but the truth; and yet, if I confine myself to the truth, I can not help fearing I shall do my profession a wrong in the minds of those who have been in the habit of considering diplomacy an occult science, as mysterious as alchemy, and as dangerous to the morals as municipal politics. It must be admitted that this conception of the diplomatic function is not without a certain historical foundation.

There was a time when diplomacy was a

science of intrigue and falsehood, of traps and mines and countermines. The word "machiavelic" has become an adjective in our common speech, signifying fraudulent craft and guile; but Machiavel was as honest a man as his time justified or required. The King of Spain wrote to the King of France after the massacre of St. Bartholomew congratulating him upon the splendid dissimulation with which that stroke of policy had been accomplished. In the last generation it was thought a remarkable advance in straightforward diplomacy when Prince Bismarck recognized the advantage of telling the truth, even at the risk of misleading his adversary. It may be another instance of that naïf credulity with which I have often been charged by European critics when I say that I really believe the world has moved onward in diplomacy as in many other matters. In my experience of diplomatic life, which now covers more years than I like to look back upon, and in the far greater record of American diplomacy which I have read and studied, I can say without hesitation that we have generally told squarely what we wanted, announced early in negotiation what we were willing to give, and allowed the other side to accept or reject our terms. During the time in which I have been prominently concerned in our foreign relations, I can also say that we have been met by the representatives of other powers in the same spirit of frankness and sincerity. You, as men of large affairs, will bear me out in saying there is nothing like straightforwardness to beget its like.

The comparative simplicity of our diplomatic methods would be a matter of necessity if it were not of choice. Secret treaties, reserved clauses, private understandings, are impossible to us. No treaty has any validity until ratified by the Senate; many require the action of both Houses of Congress to be carried into effect. They must, therefore, be in harmony with public opinion. The Executive could not change this system, even if he should ever desire to. It must be accepted, with all its difficulties and all its advantages; and it has been approved by the experience of a hundred years.

As to the measure of success which our recent diplomacy has met with, it is difficult, if not impossible, for me to speak. There are two important lines of human endeavor in which men are forbidden even to allude to their success—affairs of the heart and diplomatic affairs. In doing so, one not only commits a vulgarity which transcends all question of taste, but makes all future success impossible. For this reason, the diplomatic representatives of the Government must frequently suffer in silence the most outrageous imputations upon their patriotism, their intelligence, and their common honesty. To justify themselves before the public, they would sometimes have to place in jeopardy the interests of the nation. They must constantly adopt for themselves the motto of the French revolutionist, "Let my name wither, rather than my country be injured."

But if we are not permitted to boast of what we have done, we can at least say a word about what we have tried to do, and the principles which have guided our action. The briefest expression of our rule of conduct is, perhaps, the Monroe Doctrine and the Golden Rule. With this simple chart we can hardly go far wrong.

I think I may say that our sister republics to the south of us are perfectly convinced of the sincerity of our attitude. They know we desire the prosperity of each of them, and peace and harmony among them. We no more want their territory than we covet the mountains of the moon. We are grieved and distressed when there are differences among them, but even then we should never think of trying to compose any of those differences unless by the request of both parties. Not even our earnest desire for peace among them will lead us to any action which might offend their national dignity or their just sense of independence. We owe them all the consideration which we claim for ourselves. To critics in various climates who have other views of our purposes we can only wish fuller information and more quiet consciences.

As to what we have tried to do—what we are still trying to do—in the general field of diplomacy, there is no reason for doubt on the one hand or reticence on the other. President McKinley in his messages during the last four years has made the subject perfectly clear. We have striven, on the lines laid down by Washington, to cultivate friendly relations with all powers, but not to take part in the formation of groups or combinations among them. A position of complete independence is not incompatible with relations involving not friendship alone, but concurrent action as well in important emergencies. We have kept always in view the fact that we are preëminently a peace-loving people; that our normal activities are in the direction of trade and commerce; that the vast development of our industries imperatively demands that we shall not only retain and confirm our hold on our present markets, but seek constantly, by all honorable means, to extend our commercial interests in every practicable direction. It is for this reason we have negotiated the treaties of reciprocity which now await the action of the Senate; all of them conceived in the traditional American spirit of protection to our own industries, and yet mutually advantageous to ourselves and our neighbors. In the same spirit we have sought, successfully, to induce all the great powers to unite in a recognition of the general principle of equality of commercial access and opportunity in the markets of the Orient. We believe that "a fair field and no favor" is all we require; and with less than that we can not be satisfied. If we accept the assurances we have received as honest and genuine, as I certainly do, that equality will not be denied us; and the result may safely be left to American genius and energy.

We consider our interests in the Pacific Ocean as great now as those of any other power, and destined to indefinite development. We have opened our doors to the people of Hawaii; we have accepted the responsibility of the Philippines which Providence imposed upon us; we have put an end to the embarrassing condominium in which we were involved in Samoa, and while abandoning none of our commercial rights in the entire group, we have established our flag and our authority in Tutuila, which gives us the finest harbor in the South Seas. Next in order will come a Pacific cable, and an isthmian canal for the use of all well-disposed peoples, but under exclusive American ownership and American control—of both of which great enterprises President McKinley and President Roosevelt have been the energetic and consistent champions.

Sure as we are of our rights in these matters, convinced as we are of the authenticity of the vision which has led us thus far and still beckons us forward, I can yet assure you that so long as the administration of your affairs remains in hands as strong and skillful as those to which they have been and are now confided, there will be no more surrender of our rights than there will be violation of the rights of others. The President to whom you have given your invaluable trust and confidence, like his now immortal predecessor, is as incapable of bullying a strong power as he is of wronging a weak one. He feels and knows—for has he not tested it, in the currents of the heady fight, as well as in the toilsome work of administration?—that the nation over whose destinies he presides has a giant's strength in the works of war, as in the works of peace. But that consciousness of strength brings with it no temptation to do injury to any power on earth, the proudest or the humblest. We frankly confess we seek the friendship of all the powers; we want to trade with all peoples; we are conscious of resources that will make our commerce a source of advantage to them and of profit to ourselves. But no wantonness of strength will ever induce us to drive a hard bargain with another nation because it is weak, nor will any fear of ignoble criticism tempt us to insult or defy a great power because it is strong, or even because it is friendly.

The attitude of our diplomacy may be indicated in a text of Scripture which Franklin—the first and greatest of our diplomats—tells us passed through his mind when he was presented at the Court of Versailles. It was a text his father used to quote to him in the old candle shop in Boston, when he was a boy: "Seest thou a man diligent in his business, he shall stand before kings." Let us be diligent in our business and we shall stand—stand, you see, not crawl, nor swagger—stand, as a friend and equal, asking nothing, putting up with nothing but what is right and just, among our peers, in the great democracy of nations.

A FESTIVAL OF PEACE

ADDRESS BEFORE THE NATIONAL EDITORIAL ASSOCIATION, PAN AMERICAN EXPOSITION, BUFFALO, JUNE 13th, 1901

A FESTIVAL OF PEACE

LAST night, as I looked from my window at this marvelous creation, lined in fire upon the evening sky, and to-day, as I have walked through the courts and the palaces of this incomparable exhibition, the words of the prophet have been constantly in my mind: "Your old men shall dream dreams; your young men shall see visions." We who are old have through many hopeful years dreamed this dream. It was noble and inspiring, leading to earnest and uplifting labor. And now we share with you who are young the pleasures of beholding the vision, far nobler and more inspiring than the dream.

This ideal of the brotherhood of the nations of the Western World is not a growth of yesterday. It was heralded when the country was young by the clarion voice of Henry Clay; it was cherished by Seward and Evarts, by Douglas and by Blaine.

Twelve years ago we held the first reunion of the American republics. Much was said and done, destined to be memorable in our history, opening and blazing the way along the path of peace and fraternal relations. We have made steady progress; we have grown from day to day to a better understanding, until now we are looking to our coming conference in the City of Mexico, in which we have the right to hope that with larger experience and profounder study of the great problems before us results still more important and beneficial will be reached.

As a means to these ends, as a concrete realization of those generous dreams which have led us thus far, we have this grand and beautiful spectacle, never to be forgotten, a delight to the eyes, a comfort to every patriot heart that, during the coming summer, shall make the joyous pilgrimage to this enchanted scene, where lake and shore and sky, the rich, bright city throbbing with vigorous life, and in the distance the flash and the roar of the stupendous cataract unite their varied attractions in one charm of powerful magic such as the world has seldom seen.

There have been statesmen and soldiers who have cherished the fancy in past years of a vast American army recruited from every country between the Arctic and the Antarctic seas, which should bind us together in one immense military power that might overawe the older civilization. But this conception belongs to the past, to an order of things that has gone, I hope, forever. How far more inspiring is the thought of the results we have here now! How much more in keeping with the better times in whose light we live, and the still more glorious future to which we look forward, is the result we see to-day of the armies of labor and intelligence in every country of this New World, all working with one mind and one will, not to attain an unhappy pre-eminence in the art of destruction, but to advance in liberal emulation in the arts which tend to make this long-harassed and tormented earth a brighter and more blest abode for men of good will!

Our hearts have glowed within us as we have surveyed at every turn the evidences of the equality and fraternity of progress under skies so distant, under conditions so varying, as those which obtain between Alaska, and Cape Horn. I remember how, at a World's Fair in Paris, a great writer exclaimed: "What a prodigious amount of intelligence there is in the world!" We can say, with hearts full of gratitude and pride: How prodigious is the progress of intelligence and industry in this New World of ours!

All the triumphs of the spirit and of the skilled hands of labor, the garnered treasures of science, the witcheries of art, the spoils of earth and air and sea are gathered here to warn, to delight, to encourage and reward the ever-striving, the indomitable mind of man. Here you have force, which enables men to conquer and tame the powers of nature; wealth, not meant, as Tennyson sang, to rest in moulded heaps, but smit with the free light to melt and fatten lower lands; beauty, not for the selfish gratification of the few, but for the joy of the many to fill their days with gladness and their nights with music; and, hovering over all, the sublime, the well-nigh divine conception of a brotherhood of mutually helpful nations, fit harbinger and forerunner of a brotherhood of man.

God forbid that there should be in all this the slightest hint of vain glory, still less of menace to the rest of the world. On the contrary, we cannot but think that this friendly challenge we send out to all peoples, convoking them also to join in this brotherly emulation, in which the prizes are, after all, merely the right to further peaceful progress in good work, will be to the benefit and profit of every country under the wide heaven.

Every great achievement in art, in science, in commerce, communicates to the universal human spirit a salutary shock which in ever-widening circles spreads to regions the most remote and obscure, to break at last in lingering ripples on the ultimate shores of space and time. Out of a good source evil cannot flow; out of the light darkness cannot be born. The benignant influences that shall emanate from this great festival of peace shall not be bounded by oceans nor by continents.

WILLIAM McKINLEY

MEMORIAL ADDRESS BY INVITATION OF THE CONGRESS
DELIVERED IN THE CAPITOL AT WASHINGTON
FEBRUARY 27th, 1902

WILLIAM McKINLEY

FOR the third time the Congress of the United States are assembled to commemorate the life and the death of a President slain by the hand of an assassin. The attention of the future historian will be attracted to the features which reappear with startling sameness in all three of these awful crimes: the uselessness, the utter lack of consequence of the act; the obscurity, the insignificance of the criminal; the blamelessness—so far as in our sphere of existence the best of men may be held blameless—of the victim. Not one of our murdered Presidents had an enemy in the world; they were all of such pre-eminent purity of life that no pretext could be given for the attack of passional crime; they were all men of democratic instincts who could never have offended the most jealous advocates of equality; they were of kindly and generous nature, to whom wrong or injustice was impossible; of moderate fortune, whose slender means nobody could envy. They were men of austere virtue, of tender heart, of eminent abilities, which they had devoted with single minds to the good of the Republic. If ever men walked before God and man without blame, it was these three rulers of our people. The only temptation to attack their lives offered was their gentle radiance—to eyes hating the light that was offense enough.

The stupid uselessness of such an infamy affronts the common sense of the world. One can conceive how the death of a dictator may change the political conditions of an Empire; how the extinction of a narrowing line of kings may bring in an alien dynasty. But in a well-ordered Republic like ours, the ruler may fall, but the State feels no tremor. Our beloved and revered leader is gone—but the natural process of our laws provides us a successor identical in purpose and ideals, nourished by the same teachings, inspired by the same principles, pledged by tender affection as well as by high loyalty to carry to completion the immense task committed to his hands, and to smite with iron severity every manifestation of that hideous crime which his mild predecessor, with his dying breath, forgave. The sayings of celestial wisdom have no date; the words that reach us, over two thousand years, out of the darkest hour of gloom the world has ever known, are true to the life to-day: "They know not what they do." The blow struck at our dear friend and ruler was as deadly as blind hate could make it; but the blow struck at anarchy was deadlier still.

What a world of insoluble problems such an event excites in the mind! Not merely in its personal, but in its public aspects, it presents a paradox not to be comprehended. Under a system of government so free and so impartial that we recognize its existence only by its benefactions; under a social order so purely democratic that classes can not exist in it, affording opportunities so universal that even conditions are as changing as the winds, where the laborer of to-day is the capitalist of to-morrow; under laws which are the result of ages of evolution, so uniform and so beneficent that the President has just the same rights and privileges as the artisan; we see the same hellish growth of hatred and murder which dogs equally the footsteps of benevolent monarchs and blood-stained despots. How many countries can join with us in the community of a kindred sorrow! I will not speak of those distant regions where assassination enters into the daily life of government. But among the nations bound to us by the ties of familiar intercourse—who can forget that wise and high-minded Autocrat who had earned the proud title of the Liberator? that enlightened and magnanimous citizen whom France still mourns? that brave and chivalrous King of Italy who only lived for his people? and, saddest of all, that lovely and sorrowing Empress, whose harmless life could hardly have excited the animosity of a demon. Against that devilish spirit nothing avails—neither virtue, nor patriotism, nor age nor youth, nor conscience nor pity. We can not even say that education is a sufficient safeguard against this baleful evil—for most of the wretches whose crimes have so shocked humanity in recent years are men not unlettered, who have gone from the common schools, through murder, to the scaffold.

Our minds can not discern the origin, nor conceive the extent of wickedness so perverse and so cruel; but this does not exempt us from the duty of trying to control and counteract it. We do not understand what electricity is; whence it comes or what its hidden properties may be. But we know it as a mighty force for good or evil—and so with the painful toil of years, men of learning and skill have labored to store and to subjugate it, to neutralize, and even to employ its destructive energies. This problem of anarchy is dark and intricate, but it ought to be within the compass of democratic government—although no sane mind can fathom the mysteries of these untracked and orbitless natures—to guard against their aberrations, to take away from them the hope of escape, the long luxury of scandalous days in court, the unwholesome sympathy of hysterical degenerates, and so by degrees to make the crime not worth committing, even to these abnormal and distorted souls.

It would be presumptuous for me in this presence to suggest the details of remedial legislation for a malady so malignant. That task may safely be left to the skill and patience of the National Congress, which have never been found unequal to any such emergency. The country believes that the memory of three murdered comrades of yours—all of whose voices still haunt these walls—will be a sufficient inspiration to enable you to solve even this abstruse and painful problem, which has dimmed so many pages of history with blood and with tears.

Before an audience less sympathetic than this, I should not dare to speak of that great career which we have met to commemorate. But we are all his friends, and friends do not criticize each other's words about an open grave. I thank you for the honor you have done me in inviting me here, and not less for the kind forbearance I know I shall have from you in my most inadequate efforts to speak of him worthily.

The life of William McKinley was, from his birth to his death, typically American. There is no environment, I should say, anywhere else in the world which could produce just such a character. He was born into that way of life which elsewhere is called the middle class, but which in this country is so nearly universal as to make of other classes an almost negligible quantity. He was neither rich nor poor, neither proud nor humble; he knew no hunger he was not sure of satisfying, no luxury which could enervate mind or body. His parents were sober, God-fearing people; intelligent and upright; without pretension and without humility. He grew up in the company of boys like himself; wholesome, honest, self-respecting. They looked down on nobody; they never felt it possible they could be looked down upon. Their houses were the homes of probity, piety, patriotism. They learned in the admirable school readers of fifty years ago the lessons of heroic and splendid life which have come down from the past. They read in their weekly newspapers the story of the world's progress, in which they were eager to take part, and of the sins and wrongs of civilization with which they burned to do battle. It was a serious and thoughtful time. The boys of that day felt dimly, but deeply, that days of sharp struggle and high achievement were before them. They looked at life with the wondering yet resolute eyes of a young esquire in his vigil of arms. They felt a time was coming when to them should be addressed the stern admonition of the Apostle, "Quit you like men; be strong."

It is not easy to give to those of a later generation any clear idea of that extraordinary spiritual awakening which passed over the country at the first red signal fires of the Civil War. It was not our earliest apocalypse; a hundred years before the nation had been revealed to itself, when after long discussion and much searching of heart the people of the colonies had resolved that to live without liberty was worse than to die, and had therefore wagered in the solemn game of war "their lives, their fortunes, and their sacred honor." In a stress of heat and labor unutterable, the country had been hammered and welded together; but thereafter for nearly a century there had been nothing in our life to touch the innermost fountain of feeling and devotion; we had had rumors of wars—even wars we had had, not without sacrifices and glory—but nothing which went to the vital self-consciousness of the country, nothing which challenged the nation's right to live. But in 1860 the nation was going down into the Valley of Decision.

The question which had been debated on

thousands of platforms, which had been discussed in countless publications, which, thundered from innumerable pulpits, had caused in their congregations the bitter strife and dissension to which only cases of conscience can give rise, was everywhere pressing for solution. And not merely in the various channels of publicity was it alive and clamorous. About every fireside in the land, in the conversation of friends and neighbors, and, deeper still, in the secrecy of millions of human hearts, the battle of opinion was waging; and all men felt and saw—with more or less clearness—that an answer to the importunate question, Shall the nation live? was due, and not to be denied. And I do not mean that in the North alone there was this austere wrestling with conscience. In the South as well, below all the effervescence and excitement of a people perhaps more given to eloquent speech than we were, there was the profound agony of question and answer, the summons to decide whether honor and freedom did not call them to revolution and war. It is easy for partisanship to say that the one side was right and that the other was wrong. It is still easier for an indolent magnanimity to say that both were right. Perhaps in the wide view of ethics one is always right to follow his conscience, though it lead him to disaster and death. But history is inexorable. She takes no account of sentiment and intention; and in her cold and luminous eyes that side is right which fights in harmony with the stars in their courses. The men are right through whose efforts and struggles the world is helped onward, and humanity moves to a higher level and a brighter day.

The men who are living to-day and who were young in 1860 will never forget the glory and glamour that filled the earth and the sky when the long twilight of doubt and uncertainty was ending and the time of action had come. A speech by Abraham Lincoln was an event not only of high moral significance, but of far-reaching importance; the drilling of a militia company by Ellsworth attracted national attention; the fluttering of the flag in the clear sky drew tears from the eyes of young men. Patriotism, which had been a rhetorical expression, became a passionate emotion, in which instinct, logic, and feeling were fused.

The country was worth saving; it could be saved only by fire; no sacrifice was too great; the young men of the country were ready for the sacrifice; come weal, come woe, they were ready.

At seventeen years of age William McKinley heard this summons of his country. He was the sort of youth to whom a military life in ordinary times would possess no attractions. His nature was far different from that of the ordinary soldier. He had other dreams of life, its prizes and pleasures, than that of marches and battles. But to his mind there was no choice or question. The banner floating in the morning breeze was the beckoning gesture of his country. The thrilling notes of the trumpet called *him*—him and none other—into the ranks. His portrait in his first uniform is familiar to you all—the short, stocky figure; the quiet, thoughtful face; the deep, dark eyes. It is the face of a lad who could not stay at home when he thought he was needed in the field. He was of the stuff of which good soldiers are made. Had he been ten years older he would have entered at the head of a company and come out at the head of a division. But he did what he could. He enlisted as a private; he learned to obey. His serious, sensible ways, his prompt, alert efficiency soon attracted the attention of his superiors. He was so faithful in little things they gave him more and more to do. He was untiring in camp and on the march; swift, cool, and fearless in fight. He left the army with field rank when the war ended, brevetted by President Lincoln for gallantry in battle.

In coming years when men seek to draw the moral of our great Civil War nothing will seem to them so admirable in all the history of our two magnificent armies as the way in which the war came to a close. When the Confederate army saw the time had come, they acknowledged the pitiless logic of facts, and ceased fighting. When the army of the Union saw it was no longer needed, without a murmur or question, making no terms, asking no return, in the flush of victory and fullness of might, it laid down its arms and melted back into the mass of peaceful citizens. There is no event, since the nation was born, which has so proved its solid capacity for self-government. Both sections share equally in that crown of glory.

They had held a debate of incomparable importance and had fought it out with equal energy. A conclusion had been reached—and it is to the everlasting honor of both sides that they each knew when the war was over, and the hour of a lasting peace had struck. We may admire the desperate daring of others who prefer annihilation to compromise, but the palm of common sense, and, I will say, of enlightened patriotism, belongs to the men like Grant and Lee, who knew when they had fought enough, for honor and for country.

William McKinley, one of that sensible million of men, gladly laid down his sword and betook himself to his books. He quickly made up the time lost in soldiering. He attacked his Blackstone as he would have done a hostile entrenchment; finding the range of a country law library too narrow, he went to the Albany Law School, where he worked energetically with brilliant success; was admitted to the bar and settled down to practice—a brevetted veteran of 24—in the quiet town of Canton, now and henceforward forever famous as the scene of his life and his place of sepulture. Here many blessings awaited him: high repute, professional success, and a domestic affection so pure, so devoted and stainless that future poets, seeking an ideal of Christian marriage, will find in it a theme worthy of their songs. This is a subject to which the lightest allusion seems profanation; but it is impossible to speak of William McKinley without remembering that no truer, tenderer knight to his chosen lady ever lived among mortal men. If to the spirits of the just made perfect is permitted the consciousness of earthly things, we may be sure that his faithful soul is now watching over that gentle sufferer who counts the long hours in their shattered home in the desolate splendor of his fame.

A man possessing the qualities with which nature had endowed McKinley seeks political activity as naturally as a growing plant seeks light and air. A wholesome ambition; a rare power of making friends and keeping them; a faith, which may be called religious, in his country and its institutions; and, flowing from this, a belief that a man could do no nobler work than to serve such a country—these were the elements in his character that drew him irresistibly into public life. He had from the beginning a remarkable equipment: a manner of singular grace and charm; a voice of ringing quality and great carrying power—vast as were the crowds that gathered about him, he reached their utmost fringe without apparent effort. He had an extraordinary power of marshaling and presenting significant facts, so as to bring conviction to the average mind. His range of reading was not wide; he read only what he might some day find useful, and what he read his memory held like brass. Those who knew him well in those early days can never forget the consummate skill and power with which he would select a few pointed facts, and, blow upon blow, would hammer them into the attention of great assemblages in Ohio, as Jael drove the nail into the head of the Canaanite captain. He was not often impassioned; he rarely resorted to the aid of wit or humor; yet I never saw his equal in controlling and convincing a popular audience by sheer appeal to their reason and intelligence. He did not flatter or cajole them, but there was an implied compliment in the serious and sober tone in which he addressed them. He seemed one of them; in heart and feeling he *was* one of them. Each workingman in a great crowd might say: That is the sort of man I would like to be, and under more favoring circumstances might have been. He had the divine gift of sympathy, which, though given only to the elect, makes all men their friends.

So it came naturally about that in 1876—the beginning of the second century of the Republic—he began, by an election to Congress, his political career. Thereafter for fourteen years this Chamber was his home. I use the word advisedly. Nowhere in the world was he so in harmony with his environment as here; nowhere else did his mind work with such full consciousness of its powers. The air of debate was native to him; here he drank delight of battle with his peers. In after days, when he drove by this stately pile, or when on rare occasions his duty called him here, he greeted his old haunts with the affectionate zest of a child of the house; during all the last ten years of his life, filled as they were with activity and glory, he never ceased to be home-sick for this Hall. When he came to the Presidency, there was not a day when his Congressional service was not of use to him. Probably no other President has been in such full and cordial communion with Congress, if we may except Lincoln alone. McKinley knew the legislative body thoroughly, its composition, its methods, its habits of thought. He had the profoundest respect for its authority and an inflexible belief in the ultimate rectitude of its purposes. Our history shows how surely an Executive courts disaster and ruin by assuming an attitude of hostility or distrust to the Legislature; and, on the other hand, McKinley's frank and sincere trust and confidence in Congress were repaid by prompt and loyal support and co-operation. During his entire term of office this mutual trust and regard—so essential to the public welfare—was never shadowed by a single cloud.

He was a Republican. He could not be anything else. A Union soldier grafted upon a Clay Whig, he necessarily believed in the "American system"—in protection to home industries; in a strong, aggressive nationality; in a liberal construction of the Constitution. What any self-reliant nation might rightly do, he felt this nation had power to do, if required by the common welfare and not prohibited by our written charter.

Following the natural bent of his mind, he

devoted himself to questions of finance and revenue, to the essentials of the national house-keeping. He took high rank in the House from the beginning. His readiness in debate, his mastery of every subject he handled, the bright and amiable light he shed about him, and above all the unfailing courtesy and good will with which he treated friend and foe alike—one of the surest signatures of a nature born to great destinies—made his service in the House a pathway of unbroken success and brought him at last to the all-important post of Chairman of Ways and Means and leader of the majority. Of the famous revenue act which, in that capacity, he framed and carried through Congress, it is not my purpose here and now to speak. The embers of the controversy in the midst of which that law had its troubled being are yet too warm to be handled on a day like this. I may only say that it was never sufficiently tested to prove the praises of its friends or the criticism of its opponents. After a brief existence it passed away, for a time, in the storm that swept the Republicans out of power. McKinley also passed through a brief zone of shadow; his Congressional district having been rearranged for that purpose by a hostile legislature.

Someone has said it is easy to love our enemies; they help us so much more than our friends. The people whose malevolent skill had turned McKinley out of Congress deserved well of him and of the Republic. Never was Nemesis more swift and energetic. The Republicans of Ohio were saved the trouble of choosing a Governor—the other side had chosen one for them. A year after McKinley left Congress he was made Governor of Ohio, and two years later he was re-elected, each time by majorities unhoped-for and overwhelming. He came to fill a space in the public eye which obscured a great portion of the field of vision. In two National Conventions, the Presidency seemed within his reach. But he had gone there in the interest of others and his honor forbade any dalliance with temptation. So his nay was nay—delivered with a tone and gesture there was no denying. His hour was not yet come.

There was, however, no long delay. He became, from year to year, the most prominent politician and orator in the country. Passionately devoted to the principles of his party, he was always ready to do anything, to go anywhere, to proclaim its ideas and to support its candidates. His face and his voice became familiar to millions of our people; and wherever they were seen and heard, men became his partisans. His face was cast in a classic mold; you see faces like it in antique marble in the galleries of the Vatican and in the portraits of the great cardinal-statesmen of Italy; his voice was the voice of the perfect orator—ringing, vibrating, tireless, persuading by its very sound, by its accent of sincere conviction. So prudent and so guarded were all his utterances, so lofty his courtesy, that he never embarrassed his friends, and never offended his opponents. For several months before the Republican National Convention met in 1896, it was evident to all who had eyes to see that Mr. McKinley was the only probable candidate of his party. Other names were mentioned, of the highest rank in ability, character, and popularity; they were supported by powerful combinations; but the nomination of McKinley as against the field was inevitable.

The campaign he made will be always memorable in our political annals. He and his friends had thought that the issue for the year was the distinctive and historic difference between the two parties on the subject of the tariff. To this wager of battle the discussions of the previous four years distinctly pointed. But no sooner had the two parties made their nominations than it became evident that the opposing candidate declined to accept the field of discussion chosen by the Republicans, and proposed to put forward as the main issue the free coinage of silver. McKinley at once accepted this challenge, and, taking the battle for protection as already won, went with energy into the discussion of the theories presented by his opponents. He had wisely concluded not to leave his home during the canvass, thus avoiding a proceeding which has always been of sinister augury in our politics; but from the front porch of his modest house in Canton he daily addressed the delegations which came from every part of the country to greet him in a series of speeches so strong, so varied, so pertinent, so full of facts briefly set forth, of theories embodied in a single phrase, that they formed the hourly text for the other speakers of his party, and give probably the most convincing proof we have of his surprising fertility of resource and flexibility of mind. All this was done without anxiety or strain. I remember a day I spent with him during that busy summer. He had made nineteen speeches the day before; that day he made many. But in the intervals of these addresses he sat in his study and talked, with nerves as quiet and a mind as free from care as if we had been spending a holiday at the seaside or among the hills.

When he came to the Presidency he confronted a situation of the utmost difficulty, which might well have appalled a man of less serene and tranquil self-confidence. There had been a state of profound commercial and industrial depression, from which his friends had said his election would relieve the country. Our relations with the outside world left much to be desired. The feeling between the Northern and Southern sections of the Union was lacking in the cordiality which was necessary to the welfare of both. Hawaii had asked for annexation and had been rejected by the preceding Administration. There was a state of things in the Caribbean which could not permanently endure. Our neighbor's house was on fire, and there were grave doubts as to our rights and duties in the premises. A man either weak or rash, either irresolute or headstrong, might have brought ruin on himself and incalculable harm to the country.

Again I crave the pardon of those who differ with me, if, against all my intentions, I happen to say a word which may seem to them unbefitting the place and hour. But I am here to give the opinion which his friends entertained of President McKinley, of course claiming no immunity from criticism in what I shall say. I believe, then, that the verdict of history will be that he met all these grave questions with perfect valor and incomparable ability; that in grappling with them he rose to the full height of a great occasion, in a manner which redounded to the lasting benefit of the country and to his own immortal honor.

The least desirable form of glory to a man of his habitual mood and temper—that of successful war—was nevertheless conferred upon him by uncontrollable events. He felt the conflict must come; he deplored its necessity; he strained almost to breaking his relations with his friends, in order, first—if it might be—to prevent and then to postpone it to the latest possible moment. But when the die was cast, he labored with the utmost energy and ardor, and with an intelligence in military matters which showed how much of the soldier still survived in the mature statesman to push forward the war to a decisive close. War was an anguish to him; he wanted it short and conclusive. His merciful zeal communicated itself to his subordinates, and the war, so long dreaded, whose consequences were so momentous, ended in a hundred days.

Mr. Stedman, the dean of our poets, has called him "Augmenter of the State." It is a noble title; if justly conferred, it ranks him among the few whose names may be placed definitely and forever in charge of the historic Muse. Under his rule Hawaii has come to us, and Tutuila; Porto Rico and the vast archipelago of the East. Cuba is free. Our position in the Caribbean is assured beyond the possibility of future question. The doctrine called by the name of Monroe, so long derided and denied by alien publicists, evokes now no challenge or contradiction when uttered to the world. It has become an international truism. Our sister republics to the south of us are convinced that we desire only their peace and prosperity. Europe knows that we cherish no dreams but those of world-wide commerce, the benefit of which shall be to all nations. The State is augmented, but it threatens no nation under heaven. As to those regions which have come under the shadow of our flag, the possibility of their being damaged by such a change of circumstances was in the view of McKinley a thing unthinkable. To believe that we could not administer them to their advantage, was to turn infidel to our American faith of more than a hundred years.

In dealing with foreign powers, he will take rank with the greatest of our diplomatists. It was a world of which he had little special knowledge before coming to the Presidency. But this marvelous adaptability was in nothing more remarkable than in the firm grasp he immediately displayed in international relations. In preparing for war and in the restoration of peace he was alike adroit, courteous, and far-sighted. When a sudden emergency declared itself, as in China, in a state of things of which our history furnished no precedent and international law no safe and certain precept, he hesitated not a moment to take the course marked out for him by considerations of humanity and the national interests. Even while the legations were fighting for their lives against bands of infuriated fanatics, he decided that we were at peace with China; and while that conclusion did not hinder him from taking the most energetic measures to rescue our imperiled citizens, it enabled him to maintain close and friendly relations with the wise and heroic viceroys of the south, whose resolute stand saved that ancient Empire from anarchy and spoliation. He disposed of every question as it arose with a promptness and clarity of vision that astonished his advisers, and he never had occasion to review a judgment or reverse a decision.

By patience, by firmness, by sheer reasonableness, he improved our understanding with all the great powers of the world, and rightly gained the blessing which belongs to the peacemakers.

But the achievements of the nation in war and diplomacy are thrown in the shade by the vast economical developments which took place during Mr. McKinley's Administration. Up to the time of his first election, the country was suffering from a long period of depression, the reasons of which I will not try to seek. But from the moment the ballots were counted that betokened his advent to power a great and momentous movement in advance declared itself along all the lines of industry and commerce. In the very month of his inauguration steel rails began to be sold at $18 a ton—one of the most significant facts of modern times. It meant that American industries had adjusted themselves to the long depression—that through the power of the race to organize and combine, stimulated by the conditions then prevailing, and perhaps by the prospect of legislation favorable to industry, America had begun to undersell the rest of the world. The movement went on without ceasing. The President and his party kept the pledges of their platform and their canvass. The Dingley bill was speedily framed and set in operation. All industries responded to the new stimulus and American trade set out on its new crusade, not to conquer the world, but to trade with it on terms advantageous to all concerned. I will not weary you with statistics; but one or two words seem necessary to show how the acts of McKinley as President kept pace with his professions as candidate. His four years of administration were costly; we carried on a war which, though brief, was expensive. Although we borrowed two hundred millions and paid our own expenses, without asking for indemnity, the effective reduction of the debt now exceeds the total of the war bonds. We pay six millions less in interest than we did before the war and no bond of the United States yields the holder 2 per cent on its market value. So much for the Government credit; and we have five hundred and forty-six millions of gross gold in the Treasury.

But, coming to the development of our trade in the four McKinley years, we seem to be entering the realm of fable. In the last fiscal year our excess of exports over imports was $664,592,826. In the last four years it was $2,354,442,213. These figures are so stupendous that they mean little to a careless reader—but consider! The excess of exports over imports for the whole preceding period from 1790 to

1897—from Washington to McKinley—was only $356,808,822.

The most extravagant promises made by the sanguine McKinley advocates five years ago are left out of sight by these sober facts. The "debtor nation" has become the chief creditor nation. The financial center of the world, which required thousands of years to journey from the Euphrates to the Thames and the Seine, seems passing to the Hudson between daybreak and dark.

I will not waste your time by explaining that I do not invoke for any man the credit of this vast result. The captain can not claim that it is he who drives the mighty steamship over the tumbling billows of the trackless deep; but praise is justly due him if he has made the best of her tremendous powers, if he has read aright the currents of the sea and the lessons of the stars. And we should be ungrateful, if in this hour of prodigious prosperity we should fail to remember that William McKinley with sublime faith foresaw it, with indomitable courage labored for it, put his whole heart and mind into the work of bringing it about; that it was his voice which, in dark hours, rang out, heralding the coming light, as over the twilight waters of the Nile the mystic cry of Memnon announced the dawn to Egypt, waking from sleep.

Among the most agreeable incidents of the President's term of office were the two journeys he made to the South. The moral reunion of the sections—so long and so ardently desired by him—had been initiated by the Spanish war, when the veterans of both sides, and their sons, had marched shoulder to shoulder together under the same banner. The President in these journeys sought, with more than usual eloquence and pathos, to create a sentiment which should end forever the ancient feud. He was too good a politician to expect any results in the way of votes in his favor, and he accomplished none. But for all that the good seed did not fall on barren ground. In the warm and chivalrous hearts of that generous people, the echo of his cordial and brotherly words will linger long, and his name will be cherished in many a household where even yet the Lost Cause is worshipped.

Mr. McKinley was re-elected by an overwhelming majority. There had been little doubt of the result among well-informed people; but when it was known, a profound feeling of relief and renewal of trust were evident among the leaders of capital and of industry, not only in this country, but everywhere. They felt that the immediate future was secure, and that trade and commerce might safely push forward in every field of effort and enterprise. He inspired universal confidence, which is the life-blood of the commercial system of the world. It began frequently to be said that such a state of things ought to continue; one after another, men of prominence said that the President was his own best successor. He paid little attention to these suggestions until they were repeated by some of his nearest friends. Then he saw that one of the most cherished traditions of our public life was in danger. The generation which has seen the prophecy of the Papal throne—*Non videbis annos Petri*—twice contradicted by the longevity of holy men was in peril of forgetting the unwritten law of our Republic: Thou shalt not exceed the years of Washington. The President saw it was time to speak, and in his characteristic manner he spoke, briefly, but enough. Where the lightning strikes there is no need of iteration. From that hour, no one dreamed of doubting his purpose of retiring at the end of his second term, and it will be long before another such lesson is required.

He felt that the harvest time was come, to garner in the fruits of so much planting and culture, and he was determined that nothing he might do or say should be liable to the reproach of a personal interest. Let us say frankly he was a party man; he believed the policies advocated by him and his friends counted for much in the country's progress and prosperity. He hoped in his second term to accomplish substantial results in the development and affirmation of those policies. I spent a day with him shortly before he started on his fateful journey to Buffalo. Never had I seen him higher in hope and patriotic confidence. He was as sure of the future of his country as the Psalmist who cried, "Glorious things are spoken of thee, thou City of God." He was gratified to the heart that we had arranged a treaty which gave us a free hand in the Isthmus. In fancy he saw the canal already built and the argosies of the world passing through it in peace and amity. He saw in the immense evolution of American trade the fulfillment of all his dreams, the reward of all his labors. He was—I need not say—an ardent protectionist, never more sincere and devoted than during these last days of his life. He regarded reciprocity as the bulwark of protection—not a breach, but a fulfillment of the law. The treaties which for four years had been preparing under his personal supervision he regarded as ancillary to the general scheme. He was opposed to any revolutionary plan of change in the existing legislation; he was careful to point out that everything he had done was in faithful compliance with the law itself.

In that mood of high hope, of generous expectation, he went to Buffalo, and there, on the threshold of eternity, he delivered that memorable speech, worthy for its loftiness of tone, its blameless morality, its breadth of view, to be regarded as his testament to the nation. Through all his pride of country and his joy of its success, runs the note of solemn warning, as in Kipling's noble hymn, "Lest we forget."

Our capacity to produce has developed so enormously and our products have so multiplied that the problem of more markets requires our urgent and immediate attention. Only a broad and enlightened policy will keep what we have. No other policy will get more. In these times of marvelous business energy and gain we ought to be looking to the future, strengthening the weak places in our industrial and commercial systems, that we may be ready for any storm or strain.

By sensible trade arrangements which will not interrupt our home production we shall extend the outlets for our increasing surplus. A system which provides a mutual exchange of commodities is manifestly essential to the continued and healthful growth of our export trade. We must not repose in fancied security that we can forever sell everything and buy little or nothing. If such a thing were possible, it would not be best for us or for those with whom we deal. . . . Reciprocity is the natural outgrowth of our wonderful industrial development under the domestic policy now firmly established. . . . The period of exclusiveness is past. The expansion of our trade and commerce is the pressing problem. Commercial wars are unprofitable. A policy of good will and friendly trade relations will prevent reprisals. Reciprocity treaties are in harmony with the spirit of the times; measures of retaliation are not.

I wish I had time to read the whole of this

wise and weighty speech; nothing I might say could give such a picture of the President's mind and character. His years of apprenticeship had been served. He stood that day past master of the art of statesmanship. He had nothing more to ask of the people. He owed them nothing but truth and faithful service. His mind and heart were purged of the temptations which beset all men engaged in the struggle to survive. In view of the revelation of his nature vouchsafed to us that day, and the fate which impended over him, we can only say in deep affection and solemn awe, "Blessed are the pure in heart, for they shall see God." Even for that vision he was not unworthy.

He had not long to wait. The next day sped the bolt of doom, and for a week after—in an agony of dread broken by illusive glimpses of hope that our prayers might be answered—the nation waited for the end. Nothing in the glorious life that we saw gradually waning was more admirable and exemplary than its close. The gentle humanity of his words, when he saw his assailant in danger of summary vengeance, "Don't let them hurt him"; his chivalrous care that the news should be broken gently to his wife; the fine courtesy with which he apologized for the damage which his death would bring to the great Exhibition; and the heroic resignation of his final words, "It is God's way. His will, not ours, be done," were all the instinctive expressions of a nature so lofty and so pure that pride in its nobility at once softened and enhanced the nation's sense of loss. The Republic grieved over such a son—but is proud for ever of having produced him. After all, in spite of its tragic ending, his life was extraordinarily happy. He had, all his days, troops of friends, the cheer of fame and fruitful labor; and he became, at last,

> On fortune's crowning slope,
> The pillar of a people's hope,
> The center of a world's desire.

He was fortunate even in his untimely death, for an event so tragical called the world imperatively to the immediate study of his life and character, and thus anticipated the sure praises of posterity.

Every young and growing people has to meet, at moments, the problems of its destiny. Whether the question comes, as in Egypt, from a sphinx, symbol of the hostile forces of omnipotent nature, who punishes with instant death our failure to understand her meaning; or whether it comes, as in Jerusalem, from the Lord of Hosts, who commands the building of His temple, it comes always with the warning that the past is past, and experience vain. "Your fathers, where are they? and the prophets, do they live forever?" The fathers are dead; the prophets are silent; the questions are new, and have no answer but in time.

When the horny outside case which protects the infancy of a chrysalis nation suddenly bursts, and, in a single abrupt shock, it finds itself floating on wings which had not existed before, whose strength it has never tested, among dangers it can not foresee and is without experience to measure, every motion is a problem, and every hesitation may be an error. The past gives no clue to the future. The fathers, where are they? and the prophets, do they live forever? We are ourselves the fathers! We are ourselves the prophets! The questions that are put to us we must answer without delay, without help—for the sphinx allows no one to pass.

At such moments we may be humbly grateful to have had leaders simple in mind, clear in vision—as far as human vision can safely extend—penetrating in knowledge of men, supple and flexible under the strains and pressures of society, instinct with the energy of new life and untried strength, cautious, calm, and, above all, gifted in a supreme degree with the most surely victorious of all political virtues—the genius of infinite patience.

The obvious elements which enter into the fame of a public man are few and by no means recondite. The man who fills a great station in a period of change, who leads his country successfully through a time of crisis; who, by his power of persuading and controlling others, has been able to command the best thought of his age, so as to leave his country in a moral or material condition in advance of where he found it—such a man's position in history is secure. If, in addition to this, his written or spoken words possess the subtle quality which carries them far and lodges them in men's hearts; and, more than all, if his utterances and actions, while informed with a lofty morality, are yet tinged with the glow of human sympathy, the fame of such a man will shine like a beacon through the mists of ages—an object of reverence, of imitation, and of love. It should be to us an occasion of solemn pride that in the three great crises of our history such a man was not denied us. The moral value to a nation of a renown such as Washington's and Lincoln's and McKinley's is beyond all computation. No loftier ideal can be held up to the emulation of ingenuous youth. With such examples we can not be wholly ignoble. Grateful as we may be for what they did, let us be still more grateful for what they were. While our daily being, our public policies, still feel the influence of their work, let us pray that in our spirits their lives may be voluble, calling us upward and onward.

There is not one of us but feels prouder of his native land because the august figure of Washington presided over its beginnings; no one but vows it a tenderer love because Lincoln poured out his blood for it; no one but must feel his devotion for his country renewed and kindled when he remembers how McKinley loved, revered, and served it, showed in his life how a citizen should live, and in his last hour taught us how a gentleman could die.

AT THE UNIVERSITIES

HARVARD—PRINCETON—CALIFORNIA

AT THE UNIVERSITIES

ON RECEIVING THE DEGREE OF DOCTOR OF LAWS, HARVARD UNIVERSITY, JUNE 25th, 1902

A SCIENTIFIC friend was saying to me to-day that the one thing nature insists upon is equilibrium, which may be called the physical equivalent of justice. I suppose we only arrive at it by a process of oscillation; and I am led to accept this opinion by the kindness I have here received. Such occasions are perhaps intended, in the order of things, to make amends for much that public men have to meet in their daily lives. When you are too kind, it may not be unwholesome for us to consider that there are arrears to make up. If we know we have done nothing to deserve such kindness, we also know ourselves incapable of the infamies which are laid to our charge. In future, when I am unduly chastened, I shall reflect that Harvard has put to my credit a fund of supererogatory merit which may keep me solvent, in any stress of weather.

Let me say, Mr. Chairman, with profound sincerity and gratitude, that I shall always regard the honor I have received from this renowned University as my strong shield and defense against misconception from without and against discouragement from within. There is something in the complex traditions, in the accumulated intuitions of a great organism like this that seems to confer on it an extra-human power of getting at essentials, of seeing the man under his faults and follies, of taking into account, as we hope Heaven does, the intention, under all contradictions and imperfections. In the case of him with whom I was to have visited you last year, who deprived himself of the great pleasure of being here only in obedience to the highest and tenderest sense of duty, who hoped still to come to harvest your greetings, but who has received instead, from no mortal hands, peace and blessedness eternal—in his case, I say, it required no special acumen to see his deserving. It was easy to recognize that rare combination of matchless abilities and the purest purposes, and that incomparable genius for government which, united with exalted patriotism, had compelled as it will always compel, success and glory. And if I may compare a cedar on Lebanon to a weed in the wall, I will be so bold as to say that in paying me this too generous compliment, not warranted, I keenly feel, by anything I have accomplished, you have, I believe, intended to give your lofty recognition to the purpose with which I entered upon office and the motives which have so far guided me —and these, I trust, are not altogether unworthy even of the high commission you allow me to bear in your name.

I thank you, Mr. Chairman, for what you have said of my branch of the public work; we have labored under the same roof at kindred tasks; we have sat at the same council table. Now that you have promoted yourself to the superior rank of private citizenship, your intimate knowledge of the things whereof you speak makes your approval doubly grateful. The rest of us will be indeed happy if, when we go, we can leave behind us a record so substantial and so stainless. I thank all of you, gentlemen, for the kind manner in which you have received the Chairman's remarks. Perhaps I may be pardoned for saying a word in reference to the subject. There is little of the occult or the esoteric about the conduct of our diplomacy in modern times. The principles which have governed me are of limpid simplicity. We have sought in all things the interest and honor of our own country. We have never found this incompatible with a due regard for the interest and honor of other powers. We have treated all our neighbors with frankness and courtesy; we have received courtesy and frankness in return. We have set no traps; we have wasted no energy in evading the imaginary traps of others. We have sometimes been accused of credulity; but our credulity has not always gone unjustified. Once all the world said to us: "How can you believe a story so preposterous?" and a few weeks later all the world believed it, with joy and thanksgiving. There might be worse reputations for a country to acquire than that of always speaking the truth, and always expecting it from others. In bargaining we have tried not to get the worst of the deal; remembering, however, that the best bargains are those that satisfy both sides.

It must be confessed our horizon is expanding; we are now too big to shirk our fair share of responsibility; let us hope we may never be big enough to have outgrown our conscience. We owe it to our past to be true to our history; we owe it to our future not to be false to our ideals. And this we cannot be under the leadership of that militant son of Harvard who now sits in the seat of Washington whose education, begun here, has been continued in the mountains of the West, in varied and exacting civil administration, in the storm and stress of battle, and on the comely height of supreme power.

You may be sure that the fair renown of Harvard will never suffer in the hands of Theodore Roosevelt.

There are many crosses and trials in the life of one who is endeavoring to serve the commonwealth, but there are also two permanent sources of comfort. One is the support and sympathy of honest and reasonable people. The other is the conviction dwelling forever, like a well of living water, in the hearts of all of us who have faith in the country, that all we do, in the fear of God and the love of the land, will somehow be overruled to the public good;

and that even our errors and failures cannot greatly check the irresistible onward march of this mighty Republic, the consummate evolution of countless ages, called by divine voices to a destiny grander and brighter than we can conceive, and moving always, consciously or unconsciously, along lines of beneficent achievement whose constant aims and ultimate ends are peace and righteousness.

ON RECEIVING THE DEGREE OF DOCTOR OF LAWS, PRINCETON UNIVERSITY, OCTOBER 22, 1900

My gratitude for this distinguished honor is not diminished—it is rather enhanced—by the sense of my personal unworthiness of it. I accept it, Sir, with deep appreciation, for I am allowed to interpret it as a sign of your approval of the manner in which I and my colleagues in the Government—under the direction of the President—have conducted the foreign relations of the country for the past two years. They have been years of much labor and many perplexities and if any measure of success has attended our efforts, it has been due, not to any strength or ability of mine, but to the fact that our course was so clearly marked out for us by a century of national traditions, from which we have never swerved. We have believed in the country as our fathers did, in its high and beneficent destiny, and, so believing, we needed to admit no other considerations than those of the national welfare; we had to hearken to no voices but the call of duty and honor. I hope I may say—even in this presence—that the light which has guided me has been at least of kin to that "bright effluence" which has made this great University for so many generations a radiant beacon to the continent, of sound learning and pure morals. In the brief space of public service which may yet be mine, I can have no loftier inspiration than the desire to become less unworthy of the honor you have done me and the responsibility you have to-day laid upon me.

UNIVERSITY OF CALIFORNIA, BERKELEY, MAY 15, 1901

Mr. President, Ladies and Gentlemen: It is not difficult for you to appreciate the feelings of profound depression with which we, the associates of the President in this journey, appear before you to-day. He had long looked forward to the pleasure of meeting you in person; until an hour ago he had not abandoned that hope. But the serious condition of Mrs. McKinley's health has made it impossible for him to leave the city of San Francisco to-day. He charged us therefore to come in his stead, and express his profound feelings of sorrow and regret that he is not able to be with you. I can well appreciate your sense of disappointment; I hope you can sympathize a little with ours.

President McKinley would have come to you, with enthusiasm as warm as yours, with sympathies as quick as those of the youngest among you, to bring to you some of his garnered sheaves of experience and of wisdom. It is afflicting to me that I am forced to stand before you, and to plead *in forma pauperis,* with empty hands.

The President would have told you how he, as well as the rest of us, from the moment of our entrance into this wonderful State of California, has been charmed and delighted with everything he has seen and all he has met. You have, indeed, a goodly heritage. It would be hard to find in any land so much of material beauty as we have seen since we came over the mountains and deserts into these verdant valleys—marvelous in color, in fruitfulness and charm. It is a country of easy miracles. Everything is possible to such a State and such a people. Underlying all the radiant attractiveness which the outward aspect of nature everywhere displays, there is the element of force and greatness which is equally unmistakable. The beauty of California is not the "fatal gift" of which Filicaja sang in words of more melody and bitterness than perhaps ever were compressed into fourteen lines of literature. The beauty of this imperial State, instead of being a source of weakness and disaster, as that of Italy has been, through troubled centuries, to her,—is an element of strength and power. It is like the proud beauty of an Empress, gilding her crown with transcendent luster, rather than that of a peasant, which attracts the notice of a marching soldier. This mighty state, a powerful member of an invincible Union, has nothing to fear from the cupidity or envy of any passer-by. You are born to great destinies—you are fated to great fortunes. An important present is yours, a vaster future awaits you. And since I have spoken of Italy, I will refer once more to the thought, which has been much in our minds since we arrived here, of that famous aphorism of Goethe, "Beyond the Alps lies Italy." Beyond the ruggedness of the mountains, the amenity of these laughing valleys; beyond the gray waste of the desert, this paradise of fruitage and bloom. But the words of the sublime poet are still more applicable to you in a moral sense. In the march of political and social culture, your Alps are all behind you. The difficulties and dangers through which you gained your position in the world, have passed away forever. Now new and greater achievements await you, the conquests of the intellect, the victories of the spirit. And in these, as in your material development and in the onward progress of your State, you need dread no rivals, you need shrink from no competition. It is evident that among all your advantages, the greatest of all, that of public spirit, of civic pride and devotion, is not lacking. A shining proof of this is in this magnificent institution of learning, the fruit of an enlightened public policy, and of intelligent private munificence. It is impossible to set bounds to the far-reaching influence of an establishment like this and like your sister university at Palo Alto. You start, in full-statured youth, where the institutions of the old world have arrived after ages of successful effort and development. Who can compute the power for good, in all the future, of these great centers of illumination, rising full-orbed in the very dawn of your history? How profound the significance of the fact that here, at the utmost verge of this vast continent, stands an Oxford, a Cambridge, ready made!

Young men and women of California!—your Alps are passed: your Italy lies before you. You have only to enter in, and take possession of your magnificent inheritance. In the name of the President, I bid you God-speed on your way.

COMMERCIAL CLUB DINNER

PREPARED FOR THE COMMERCIAL CLUB OF CHICAGO, DECEMBER, 1904, BUT NOT DELIVERED, OWING TO THE DEATH OF A BROTHER OF MR. HAY'S

COMMERCIAL CLUB DINNER

CHICAGO, 1901

I AM glad of the privilege of expressing the heartfelt gratitude of all my associates, and my own also, for the more than princely hospitality of Chicago. We have received much kindness. We have seen many splendid sights, but Chicago itself has been the most glorious of all. I hardly believe you know how magnificent you have been during the last few days. To do the greatest things in the grandest manner, and to think little about it, seems to me the distinguishing characteristic of this wonderful place.

One of the first men of letters, one of the deepest thinkers of England, while expressing his regret that so few people in Europe had seen the greatest spectacle of modern times, the Chicago Fair, said to me: "The fault was partly in the people of Chicago. They do not advertise themselves enough." Whenever I come to Chicago I am struck anew by the justice of the observation and by the reasons for it. The fact is that such a thing is impossible; because in the first place you are too busy with other matters to give the advertising sufficient attention, and besides, no advertising could do justice to Chicago.

It is a city which has always occupied a large place in my thoughts. It is the home of many of my dearest friends. It is the great emporium of the State in which I passed the days of my childhood and my youth. It is, in a certain sense, my twin. I was born in the first year of its civic life. We were young together, but there, I am sorry to say, the parallel ends. Aurora and Tithonus were young together; but the one grew old and gray, while the other flourished in immortal beauty and youth. In the days when Chicago and I were both young, it was my lot to see a good deal of the outside world, and it was always a pleasure to me, in viewing what was most interesting and picturesque in decaying civilizations to think, by way of contrast, of the brilliant and vigorous municipality that was swiftly taking shape on the shores of Lake Michigan, unlike anything hitherto seen. I talked about it as young men will about things that interest them, and was sometimes goodnaturedly rallied on my vehement claims and large prophecies. But whenever I come here I see how far beyond the possibilities of brag are the simple facts of your marvelous growth. The boasting of the traveling man, the prophetic raptures of poets are alike inadequate. Chicago speaks for herself, in a language of her own, a language the world must learn to interpret, for Chicago is a fact in which the world is concerned.

No other city so epitomizes the prodigious strength, the unlimited promise of the country and the age. The gigantic heart of the continent seems beating and throbbing here, sending its currents of warm vitality through every vein of the country. On one side you have the prairie, levelled as by the hand of Providence for the building of an imperial city whose bounds no man can foretell: on the other, the lake, in its endless facilities for commerce, seems only an extension of the mighty mart. What is this we heard the other day of forty miles of shipping delayed by a temporary obstruction of your great water way? Your geographical position insured you greatness when the world was made; and all modern history has wrought for your prosperity. But all this peerless store of opportunity would not have availed, had it not been for the alert and indomitable spirit of your people. The aboriginal dwellers in this region were called Illini—which is by interpretation Men. It was men who built this town.

Opportunity alone never made a man or a city. "The skirts of happy chance" must be grasped with a firm hand. The man, or the municipality, fated to greatness, makes profit out of storm or sunshine, out of weal or woe, out of luck or disaster. Of the two capital events in your history, the Fire and the Fair, one an almost incalculable calamity, the other the greatest opportunity of the age, it is hard to tell which contributed most to the growth and prestige of Chicago. From the smouldering embers of that wide desolation of 1871 rose the public spirit of this stalwart town, like an invincible weapon, forged in flame and tempered with the chill of adversity, ready for any achievement. And when, in 1893, the time and the occasion met, to show whether Chicago was worthy of her immense prosperity, she seized the chance with a strength of grasp and a certainty of touch, that fixed her place at once and forever in the world of civilization. Never again could envy or malice say that this city was given too much to the pursuit of material gain. I know of no other town on earth which would have been capable of the magnanimity, the generosity to rivals, the sublime disregard of money, shown by Chicago in that year of inspiration and power. In the presence of that splendid largeheartedness, envy died; rivals became enthusiastic collaborators; and the result was worthy of the lofty qualities which produced it. It proved the fallacy of the opinion, so often expressed, that beauty in art and architecture is a symptom of decay. We saw the people of a great, young, thriving commercial community of their own initiative build at enormous expense, without prospect or hope of pecuniary profit, the most exquisitely beautiful creation the world has yet seen. Happy are all we who saw it! It bloomed in its vast white symmetry on the shore of the Lake like some divine miracle of a flower—as perfect in beauty, as transitory in duration. It passed away like a dream or an exhalation.

But it will remain in our minds among the richest of our recollections, fruitful forever of a fonder pride of country, of a deeper respect for human nature.

All these things rush to our thoughts when we come to Chicago, a city of so great a past, even in its mighty youth, and dowered with the certainty of a future so transcendent. Not only of itself, but as a type and symbol, it is worthy the serious attention of mankind. It symbolizes not merely the strength, the resources, the enterprise, the multifarious activities and intelligence of this magnificent State, of this glorious West, of this beloved and powerful Union of States; but, in its highest qualities, it is a type of all that is freest and most masterful in the spirit of the age, in the aspirations and progress of the world. It would be futile and inane to say that a community so cosmopolitan had not its shadows as well as its lights; with the universal virtues it must have the faults which are universal; it would be presumption even to say what is right and what is wrong in a system of things so complex and so portentous. The fact transcends all theory and all criticism. The discords we perceive may be parts of a stupendous harmony too great for our appreciation—a superhuman composition through all of which beats the pulse of an abounding and ever-growing life, the rhythm of a swelling song, whose leading motives are democracy, freedom and light.

NEW ORLEANS

PREPARED FOR, BUT NOT DELIVERED ON, THE OCCASION OF THE SECRETARY OF STATE'S VISIT TO NEW ORLEANS WITH PRESIDENT McKINLEY IN 1901

NEW ORLEANS

I AM glad of the opportunity to express in behalf of my colleagues, as well as my own, our grateful appreciation of the reception we have met with in this superb Southern capital. However your kindness may have exceeded in some cases our personal deserts—and I speak especially of myself,—I am sure that so far as our intentions are concerned, we have deserved your good will. I make bold to say that in a long period of observation of public affairs I have never known an Administration more anxious than the present one to promote the interests of every section of the country. I need not say where our inspiration, our directing force, comes from. If you want to see an American, body and soul, through and through, in every fibre of his being devoted to the welfare of his country—his whole country—he is your Guest this evening. And as this genial air naturally predisposes our Northern hearts to expansion and confidence I will venture to say that those of us who are with him are like him except in fame and ability. We are all Democrats, we are all Republicans, we are all Americans. We have no principles which will not equally suit the climate of Massachusetts and that of Louisiana. Perhaps, in the Department with which I am more immediately concerned, we have been working rather more in the interest of the South than in that of other sections. We have done our best to extend your markets by reciprocal treaties and other measures, and to clear away all barriers to an Isthmian Canal under American ownership and control. We have felt it was time for the South to share in the general prosperity, and we know every section will profit by what benefits one.

Will you allow me one personal word to express the pleasure with which I find myself here. My boyhood was passed on the banks of the Mississippi—but so vast is the extent of the territory traversed by this mighty river "which drains our Andes and divides a world," so cosmical is the range of climate through which it passes, that when I was young, its northern and southern regions seemed alien and strange to each other in all aspects save those of patriotic national pride. To us for a part of the year, it was white and dazzling bridge, safe as a city street for sleighing and skating; framed in by snow-clad bluffs; but we loved to think that far away to the South it flowed through a land of perpetual summer, fragrant with fruits and everblooming flowers, blessed continually with days of sunshine and nights of balm. We thought of you without envy, but with joy that your enchanted land was ours also—that we, too, had a share in your goodly heritage. All through my childhood New Orleans was to me a realm of faery, a land of dreams. And when I grew older I read with delight your history and your literature—the one filled with romance in action, the other constantly distinguished by the touch of Southern grace and Latin art. I always wanted to see for myself the beauty of this region, to study on the spot the secret of its charm. But the strong gods Fate and Circumstance continually prevented until this day. Now I have come, and found, like a famous queen of the East, that the half has never been told. I am less fortunate than Her Majesty of Sheba—as she was young and enjoyed the Oriental leisure; while I am old and in an American hurry. I shall always be glad, though, even of this tantalizing glimpse. But the one piece of advice I shall venture to give those of you who may not know the North, is, don't put off your visit too long. Come and see us while you are young—and this excludes nobody, for you all are young. I have never seen so much youth and beauty as in the last few days. Men who are contemporaries of mine, who according to the calendar and the army lists ought to be passing into the lean and slippered pantaloon, who won world-wide fame in the Sixties, men who fought Grant and Sherman to a standstill, have the looks, the spirit and the speech of boys. I can only conjecture that they have succeeded where Ponce de Leon failed in discovering the fountain of Perpetual Youth, and naturally enough, are keeping it a secret from the rest of us.

THE GRAND ARMY OF THE REPUBLIC

ADDRESS AT THE THIRTY-SIXTH NATIONAL ENCAMPMENT, G. A. R., WASHINGTON, D.C., OCTOBER 6th., 1902

THE GRAND ARMY OF THE REPUBLIC

COMRADES OF THE GRAND ARMY:

IN the name of the President and in his stead, I bid you welcome to Washington. I need not say that on every inch of American soil, wherever that starry banner waves, you are at home, and need no formal words of welcome. But especially in this capital city of the Republic you fought to preserve, you are the children of the house; the doors are always open to you. Wherever you turn, you are reminded of the history of which you are a part. From the windows of that White House the eyes of many comrades have looked upon this field whose names belong to the ages—Lincoln, Grant, Hayes, Garfield, Harrison, McKinley, and Roosevelt. In the beautiful squares other comrades salute you from the bronze horses of the monuments where your love and loyalty have placed them. Across the winding river, the heights of Arlington show the white tents of Fame's eternal camping ground, where your friends and brothers repose. And, casting its gigantic shadow over this bivouac of yours, the unequaled obelisk of Washington towers to the clouds—the loftiest structure ever reared by man in memory of the loftiest character in human history.

A peculiar interest attends this gathering. Never again shall all of us meet in a camp like this. Not often shall the youngest and strongest of us come together to renew our memories of the past, and our vows of eternal devotion to the cause to which in those distant days we swore allegiance. Thirty-seven years have passed since some of us, wearing crape on our arms and mourning in our hearts for Abraham Lincoln, saw the great Army which he loved pass before the White House in the Grand Review. Many of you marched in those dusty columns, keeping step to the rhythm of drums and trumpets which had sounded the onset in a hundred battles. The banners blew gaily out —what was left of them; they were stained with the weather of long marches; they were splendid in the rags and tatters of glorious victories. There was not much of pomp or state about that solemn march. But the men in the street that day—many of whom I have the honor of seeing before me—afforded their own country, and the rest of the world, a lesson which shall never be forgotten, though its tremendous import was not immediately perceived. In fact many inferences were drawn at the moment which the lapse of a few months found altogether false. One trained observer of events in the Old World said: "These splendid fellows will give you trouble; it is too fine a force to be disbanded easily." He reasoned from the precedents of the past, unaware that we were making new precedents. Since then the world has learned the lesson of that hour. The normal condition of the Republic is peace, but not the nerveless peace of helplessness. We do not need the overgrown armaments of Europe. Our admirable regular force, with its perfect drill and discipline, though by far the smallest in the world in proportion to population, is sufficient for our ordinary wants; but when the occasion calls, when the vital interests or the honor of the country are threatened, when the national conscience is aroused, an army will spring from the soil, so vast, so docile, so intelligent, so formidable, that it need not fear to try conclusions with any army on the face of the earth.

But that was only half the lesson; the other half was equally important—that when that citizen Army has done its work, it makes no claim, it exacts no conditions of disbandment, but melts away into the vaster body of the nation, as the foam-crested sunlit wave melts back into the profound depths of the ocean. The great host of 1865 ceased to exist as an armed force; but in every town and hamlet of the land it lived as a part of the body politic —a nucleus everywhere of courage, patriotism, and self-sacrifice. This was a new product the Republic might proudly show to the world, saying, "These be the peaceable heroes I breed from great wars."

There were many brilliant deeds done in the war that resulted in enduring fame to fortunate individual soldiers; but the disbandment of that army, flushed with victory and idolized by the country, reflected honor upon all our race, a glory in which individual claims are lost, like atoms of cloud in the crimson splendor of a stormy sunset.

For four years you showed yourselves good soldiers—equal to the best the world had seen. For thirty-seven years you have been good citizens; and who shall say in which capacity you have wrought best for the Republic? Each year you come together with thinned ranks but undiminished spirit to feed anew the undying flame upon the altar of patriotism. I should not have said your ranks are thinned, for the place of each fallen comrade is filled with a loving memory. And who can ever forget the faces which never had a chance to grow old—the brave young warriors who fell in battle and gained the prize of immortal youth? For them there is no shadow of struggle or poverty; no trouble of gray hairs or failing strength; no care of the present nor fear of the future. The unfading light of morning is forever in their eyes; the blessing of a grateful nation hallows their names. We salute them with loving tears, from which the bitterness is gone. We hear their young voices in the clear notes of the bugle and the murmur of the fluttering flags. Our answering hearts cry, "Hail and farewell, young comrades, till we meet again!"

Our fathers ordained that in this Republic there should be no distinctions; but human nature is stronger than laws, and nothing can prevent this people from showing honor to all who have deserved well of the country. Every man who has borne arms with credit has earned and is sure to receive a special measure of regard. And it is our peculiar privilege to remember that our armies and navies, regular and volunteer, have always been worthy of esteem. In distant generations, under different flags, in conflicts great and small, by land and by sea, they have always borne their part nobly. The men who fought at Louisburg beneath the meteor flag of England; the men who stood with Washington at Yorktown; with Lincoln in the Black Hawk War; with Crockett at the Alamo; with Taylor at Buena Vista; with Grant at Vicksburg; and with Lee at Appomattox were of the stuff of which not only soldiers, but citizens, are made. And in our own time the young men who stormed the hill of San Juan, and have borne our flag with such honor to the forbidden city of Pekin and the jungles of Luzon, have shown that their progenitors bred true. The men of to-day are as good Americans as the men of yesterday, and the men of to-morrow, with God's blessing, will be the same. The dominant characteristic of every American army that has ever stepped to the tap of a drum has been valor and humanity. They have—in the long run—carried nothing but good to any land they have occupied. As our comrade McKinley—of blessed memory—said: "The flag has never floated over any region but in benediction."

By order of the President of the United States, these historic grounds, the property of the Nation, are during this Encampment dedicated to your use. They will receive from your presence an added sacredness and value. In the history of the twentieth century, which is opening with such brilliant promise, not the least luminous page will treat of this meeting of the Grand Army of the Republic—soldiers and citizens whom the Republic delights to honor.

PRESIDENT ROOSEVELT

SPEECH AT OHIO SOCIETY BANQUET, NEW YORK,
JANUARY 17th, 1903

PRESIDENT ROOSEVELT

A DISTINGUISHED American some time ago leaped into unmerited fame by saying, "Some men are born great—others are born in Ohio." This is mere tautology, for a man who is born in Ohio *is* born great. I can say this—as the rest of you cannot—without the reproach of egotism, for I have suffered all my life under the handicap of not having been born in that fortunate commonwealth. Indeed, when I look back on the shifting scenes of my life, if I am not that altogether deplorable creature, a man without a country, I am, when it comes to pull and prestige, almost equally bereft, as I am a man without a state. I was born in Indiana, I grew up in Illinois, I was educated in Rhode Island, and it is no blame to that scholarly community that I know so little. I learned my law in Springfield and my politics in Washington, my diplomacy in

Europe, Asia and Africa. I have a farm in New Hampshire and desk room in the District of Columbia. When I look to the springs from which my blood descends the first ancestors I ever heard of were a Scotchman, who was half English, and a German woman, who was half French. Of my immediate progenitors, my mother was from New England and my father was from the South. In this bewilderment of origin and experience I can only put on an aspect of deep humility in any gathering of favorite sons, and confess that I am nothing but an American. After all, that is something to be thankful for. There is a story that, in the early war days, two thoughtful Mugwumps met—they were Mugwumps before the letter, for that illuminating name was not yet invented,—and one said to the other (mingling the mutual cuttle-cloud of their gloom), "We are going to the Devil." "Yes," said the other, "and we ought to be thankful we have a Devil to go to." I am glad, if I cannot boast of a State, I at least have a nation to call myself by.

And yet, where a man is born is not a matter for personal boasting. I have never met one who chose his own birthplace; but the man is indeed fortunate who chooses the right place to be married in. This Mr. Hoyt and I did—and it is, I am sure, altogether owing to that lucky chance—for lucky chances are gregarious and like to flock together—that the greatest honors of our lives have come to us to-night—that he is your President and that I am your guest.

I lived a little while in Ohio and was very happy there, but, obeying a call which seemed to me imperative, I went to Washington some twenty years ago. I might have been pardoned for thinking I had not left Ohio, for every great department of national activity and power was under the direction of a citizen of that masterful state. The President was an Ohio man, equally distinguished in character and achievements; the finances of the country were in the strong and capable hands of John Sherman; the army gladly obeyed the orders of Tecumseh Sherman, with Phil Sheridan as second in command; while at the head of our august Supreme Court sat Chief Justice Waite; the Executive, the purse, the sword and the scales of justice, all in the hands of men from a state which naturally breeds men who know how to make war, to make money and to make laws.

And as I ought, before I take my seat, to say a word at least bearing on the subject of the toast to which I am supposed to be responding —what a roll call of great names is found in the Presidents from Ohio. The two Harrisons, old and young Tippecanoe; Grant, one of those simple great men for whom history has so sure a partiality; Hayes, the ideal republican citizen; and those twins in fate and fame, so like in destiny and so different in temperament and in methods, Garfield and McKinley—all Ohio men by birth or adoption, all illustrious in peace and war, citizens and soldiers, too, without reproach.

And the list, great as it is, is still open for indefinite expansion.

But I imagine your toast referred more especially to our actual President, our young, gallant, able, brilliant President Roosevelt. I am glad to be called on to say in his absence what few men would be hardy enough to say to his face—for, like all men of high courage and manliness, he is inhospitable to flattery. In the great roll of our Presidents—all of them men of mark, of lofty character and ideals, not one name among them smirched by the slightest stain of personal corruption or wrongdoing, all of them showing to the world clean hands and high aims—he holds now, he will hold forever, a distinguished place. The most famous of German poets has said, "A talent is formed in the solitudes, a character in the torrent of the world." Our President has had the advantage of both these environments. From the cloistered life of American college boys, sheltered from the ruder currents of the world by the ramparts of wealth and gentle nurture, he passed, still very young, to the wild and free existence of the plains and the hills. In the silence of those vast solitudes men grow to full stature, when the original stuff is good. He came back to the east, bringing with him, as Tennyson sang, "the wrestling thews that throw the world." His career since then has been singularly varied. He has gone rapidly forward and upward because that was the law of his being. He does not disdain the garland of fame, but he finds his highest enjoyment in grasping the tools that fit his hand. He has his high ideal of public work set forth by the greatest teacher and ruler that ever lived, "Whosoever will be chief among you, let him be your servant."

It does not distinguish an American President to be honest, nor to be brave, nor to be intelligent, nor to be patriotic. They have all been all of these. These qualities are postulates of the position. But the nation is to be congratulated when all these desirable attributes are heightened and tinged with that ineffable light which, for want of a more descriptive term, we call genius. It is this which makes honesty a scorching flame against fraud or corruption; which makes courage an inspiration to others in battle or in council; which raises intelligence to the quick flash of intuition and patriotism to a religious fervor of consecration, and it is this which makes Theodore Roosevelt the man and the President he is.

And, finally, I, whose memories are of a generation of which few survivors remain, feel like congratulating you who are young, in the words of the dying Voltaire on the eve of the splendors and the marvels of the French revolution, which he was not to witness, "You young men are going to see fine things." In the six years which remain of President Roosevelt's term—if my arithmetic is wrong I am open to correction—you will see what a stout heart, an active mind, a vital intelligence, a wide range of experience, a passion for justice and truth and a devoted patriotism can accomplish at the head of a nation which unites the strength of a mighty youth to the political sense which is the rich inheritance of centuries of free government.

EDMUND CLARENCE STEDMAN

PREPARED FOR DELIVERY ON MR STEDMAN'S
SEVENTIETH BIRTHDAY OCTOBER 8th, 1903

EDMUND CLARENCE STEDMAN

I ESTEEM it a great privilege to be with you to-night and to be allowed to offer, if only by my presence, my tribute of affection and regard to one of my oldest and most valued friends.

I am glad to congratulate him on this cheerful anniversary; why should we not call it his Coming of Age! Certainly our felicitations have a far more sure and substantial basis than those which greet the young heir on his twenty-first birthday. In that case, how hidden in clouds, how shrouded in uncertainty is the future! No man may tell whether the days which confront the youth have more of blessing or bane, more of joy or sorrow, more of honor or disgrace. His fate is before him, her features hidden in a veil. She shows him a road, whose windings are wrapped in mist. Nothing can guarantee the exit — neither wealth, nor station, opportunity nor the devotion of friends. All these strong supports may be beaten down like weeds by the blows of Circumstance, or the stoutest defenses may be betrayed from within by a treachery of temperament. But on a birthday like this we celebrate, the years of a man's life have dropped their veils of mystery; the book is wide open for all to read; the varied landscape of the long journey is revealed by the gentle rays of the westering sun; all the shadows are left behind. Happy the man who, like our dear and honored friend, has no favors to ask of the apocalyptic light; whose life is one consistent story of noble effort and brilliant performance; who can look back on the past without a blush and forward to the unknown without a fear.

It is a life—I will not say for our friend to be proud of—for we know too well the dignified and philosophic poise of his character to associate with it any idea of vainglory,—but it is a record and career of which his friends are justly proud. He was born a poet and he has lived faithful to the goddess; but you would seek in vain for any sign of poetic license in his life. He has shown that the highest gifts are compatible with the most rigorous industry, the most stainless honor. He has never turned away from his ideals, nor has he ever despised the homely virtues of our workaday world. Great poet, honorable man, good citizen,—what better lot could any mother pray for at the cradle of her child?

I began to hear of Stedman while he was hardly more than a boy, at a time when perhaps we thought more of the things of the spirit than we do now. The great Boston choir of poets was then in its meridian splendor; a younger trio were singing in the Middle States, Taylor, Stoddard and Boker, differing widely in character and circumstances but bound together in true friendship and a genuine love of Poesy, as they liked to call it—and after these, with the light of an auspicious dawn on their shining foreheads, came the three young heirs of fame, Stedman and Aldrich and Howells. All the others have gone to their celestial rewards, but these three are happily with us to enjoy the sweetness of a righteous renown in the land of the living.

I remember how in an hour Stedman grew famous with that Tyrtæan ballad which rang like a reveille in the troubled and clouded morning of the great war, where the poet's voice gave forth the deep inspiration of the prophet. It was when the scaffold was building for John Brown. I have not lost the sonorous refrain in forty years:

> "But, Virginians, don't do it, for I tell you that
> the flagon
> Filled with blood of John Brown's offspring was
> first poured by Southern hands,
> And each drop of old Brown's blood, like the red
> gore of the dragon,
> Shall flame a vengeful fury hissing through your
> wasted lands,
> And Old Brown—
> Ossawatomie Brown—
> Will trouble you more than ever when you've
> nailed his coffin down."

It is not given to many prophets to read their prophecies, transferred from the future to the perfect tense, in the history of their times.

As Mr. Stedman began, so he continued. There has not been a year of his life in which he has not done some good and permanent work in literature, made some conscientious and valuable contribution to criticism, borne some brave and cogent testimony in behalf of good taste, good morals and good citizenship. The standards of this country in letters and in life are higher because he has lived.

We offer him, on this day on which he begins what Victor Hugo called *la jeunesse de la vieillesse,* our heartfelt congratulations, in which love, admiration and gratitude are mingled, for all he has done and for all that he is.

LINCOLN'S FAITH

REMARKS, FROM PRESIDENT LINCOLN'S PEW, ON THE ONE-HUNDREDTH ANNIVERSARY OF THE ESTABLISHMENT OF THE NEW YORK AVENUE PRESBYTERIAN CHURCH, WASHINGTON, D. C., JUSTICE HARLAN PRESIDING, AND PRESIDENT ROOSEVELT BEING ONE OF THE SPEAKERS, NOVEMBER 16th, 1902

LINCOLN'S FAITH

MR. PRESIDENT, Mr. Justice: Ladies and Gentlemen: I could not find it in my heart to detain you, at this hour, even for a moment, by any words of mine. But perhaps you may consider that you have time to listen to one or two phrases uttered in this city many years ago by that great man to whom Mr. Justice Harlan has just alluded. Some of you, I am sure, share with me the memories to which this occasion and place give rise, of the days when I have sat in this church with that illustrious patriot whose fame even now has turned to something remote and legendary. But whatever is remembered or whatever lost, we ought never to forget that Abraham Lincoln, one of the mightiest masters of statecraft that history has known, was also one of the most devoted and faithful servants of Almighty God who has ever sat in the high places of the world. From that dim and chilly dawn when, standing on a railway platform at Springfield half veiled by falling snowflakes from the crowd of friends and neighbors who had gathered to wish him God-speed on his momentous journey, he acknowledged his dependence on God and asked for their prayers, to that sorrowful yet triumphant hour when he went to his account, he repeated over and over in every form of speech, his faith and trust in that Almighty Power who rules the fate of men and of nations. To a Committee of Presbyterians who visited him in 1863, he said: "It has been my happiness to receive testimonies of a similar nature from, I believe, all denominations of Christians. This to me is most gratifying, because from the beginning I saw that the issues of our great struggle depended on the Divine interposition and favor." A year later he said, among other things, to a Committee of the General Conference of the Methodist Church: "God bless the Methodist Church; bless all the Churches, and blessed be God who in this our great trial giveth us the Churches." I will not multiply extracts from those hundreds of public utterances, nor will I quote the sublime words of the Second Inaugural which sound like a new chapter of Hebrew prophecy; as these might be classed among the official speeches of rulers which recognize the power for good of the ordinary relations between religion and wise government. But I will ask you—and this shall be my last word—to listen to a few sentences in which Mr. Lincoln admits us into the most secret recesses of his soul. It is a meditation written in September 1862. Perplexed and afflicted beyond the power of human help, by the disasters of war, the wrangling of parties, and the inexorable and constraining logic of his own mind, he shut out the world one day, and tried to put into form his double sense of responsibility to human duty and Divine Power; and this was the result. It shows—as has been said in another place—the awful sincerity of a perfectly honest soul, trying to bring itself into closer communion with its Maker.

"The will of God prevails. In great contests each party claims to act in accordance with the will of God. Both *may* be and one *must* be wrong. God cannot be *for* and *against* the same thing at the same time. In the present civil war it is quite possible that God's purpose is something different from the purpose of either party; and yet the human instrumentalities, working just as they do, are of the best adaptation to effect His purpose. I am almost ready to say that this is probably true; that God wills this contest, and wills that it shall not end yet. By His mere great power on the minds of the now contestants, He could have either *saved* or *destroyed* the Union without a human contest. Yet the contest began. And having begun, He could give the final victory to either side any day. Yet the contest proceeds."

THE PRESS AND MODERN PROGRESS

ADDRESS AT THE OPENING OF THE PRESS PARLIAMENT OF THE WORLD, AT THE LOUISIANA PURCHASE EXPOSITION, ST. LOUIS, MAY 19th, 1904

THE PRESS AND MODERN PROGRESS

I THANK you, Mr. Chairman; I thank you, gentlemen—all of you—for your too generous and amiable welcome. I esteem it a great privilege to meet so many representatives of an estate which, more than any other, at this hour controls the world. It is my daily duty in Washington to confer with the able and distinguished representatives of civilized sovereigns and states. But we are all aware that the days of personal government are gone forever; that behind us, and behind the rulers we represent, there stands the vast, irresistible power of public opinion, which in the last resort must decide all the questions we discuss, and whose judgment is final. In your persons I greet the organs and exponents of that tremendous power with all the respect which is due to you and your constituency, deeply sensible of the honor which has been done me in making me the mouthpiece of the sentiment of appreciation and regard with which the nation welcomes you to this great festival of peace and of progress.

It is possible—if you will pardon a personal word from me—that the circumstances of my life may have commended me to the notice of President Francis, and may have led him to invite me here to-night to take part in this occasion in the dual capacity of host and guest. My years of newspaper work might entitle me to a modest place in your membership, while the valley of the mighty river which rolls by the wharves of St. Louis can never be considered by me otherwise than as my home. The years of my boyhood were passed on the banks of the Mississippi, and the great river was the scene of my early dreams. The boys of my day led an amphibious life in and near its waters in the summer time, and in the winter its dazzling ice bridge, of incomparable beauty and purity, was our favorite playground; while our imaginations were busy with the glamour and charm of the distant cities of the South, with their alluring French names and their legends of stirring adventure and pictures of perpetual summer. It was a land of faëry, alien to us in all but a sense of common ownership and patriotic pride. We built snow forts and called them the Alamo; we sang rude songs of the cane-brake and the cornfield; and the happiest days of the year to us who dwelt on the northern bluffs of the river were those that brought us, in the loud puffing and whistling steamers of the olden time, to the Mecca of our rural fancies, the bright and busy metropolis of St. Louis.

The historical value of the Mississippi is not less than its geographical and natural importance. Its course through the pages of our country's story is as significant as the tremendous sweep of its waters from the crystal lakes which sleep beneath the northern stars to the placid expanse of the Gulf of Mexico. Its navigation was a prize fiercely contended for by every chancellery of western Europe. Many suitors have looked upon it since that gallant Prince Charming, Hernando de Soto, parted the curtains of its repose, and all have found it fair. It aroused equally the interest of the Briton, the Iberian, and the Gaul. When by virtue of one of the strangest caprices of the great game of diplomacy ever known, it became our cherished possession, it gave rise to the fiercest political contests, the most far-reaching combinations. When the accumulated passions and purposes of a hundred years at last burst forth in a tempest of war, it became the center of a world's breathless interest and was flooded with the fatal and terrible light which plays about the battlefields of fame and "shines in the sudden making of splendid names." So long as its waters roll to the sea, so long will the world remember the high resolution with which Grant and Sherman hewed their way southward and the chivalrous courage with which Johnston and Pemberton opposed them. So immense is the value of that silver bar that binds together the framework of the wedded States.

We celebrate this year, with the generous assistance of a friendly world, the most important event in the history of this great valley, an event which in far-reaching and lasting results is surpassed by few in the life of the nation. It is perhaps true that to the philosophic mind all periods are critical—that every hour is the end of an era and the beginning of a new order of ages. But to us ordinary observers there occur from time to time crises in history when the line of cleavage between the old and the new is clear and distinct, where the aloe blooms, where the avalanche leaves the mountain top, where the leisurely march of events is quickened to the dynamic rush of irresistible destiny. The transfer of this imperial domain from European to American control was one of those transactions which render the period of their accomplishment memorable for all time. In no other act did the men who made the Revolution—"men," as Lowell called them, "with empires in their brains"—more clearly show their marvelous prophetic insight. The United States was, in 1803, a feeble folk, with hardly enough population to occupy the long Atlantic seacoast; with the great spaces of the Middle West scarcely yet picketed by adventurous pioneers; with imperfect means of defense against a world which still looked askance at the half-known upstart which might prove dangerous hereafter; with the heavy cares incident to the building of a new nation upon yet untried foundations. But weighty as were their responsibilities they did not hesitate to assume others weightier still. To an undeveloped empire they seized the occasion to add another still wilder and more remote. Upon their half-finished task they undauntedly superimposed another full of exacting and perilous possibilities. In their robust faith in the future—their fearless confidence in the force of the new democracy—difficulties were not considered and the impossible did not exist. To men of that strain, in an enterprise which promised usefulness and glory, toil and danger were only irresistible attractions.

While we should give due credit to the individual instrumentalities by which this great transaction was brought about, we should not forget the overwhelming influence exerted by the unseen Director of the Drama. Whether we call it the spirit of the age, or historic necessity, or the balance of power, or whether we reverently recognize in the matter the hand of that Providence which watched over our infancy as a people, we can not but admit that the acquisition of this vast territory was, in one way or another, sure to come. A wise diplomacy hastened it; a timid conservatism might have delayed it; but it was written in our horoscope. The surest proof of this lies in the eminent personalities by whom the purchase and sale were made. Jefferson was the last man in America of whom we could have expected this departure on the field of illimitable expansion, and Napoleon was, of all the sovereigns of Europe, the least likely to give up so vast an extent of empire.

One of the most brilliant and tenacious dreams of Bonaparte was to establish on the right bank of the Mississippi a Latin empire reaching from the Gulf to the Pacific Ocean, extending in future ages the glories of France to the sunset seas. The principle dearest to the heart of Jefferson was that of a strict construction of the Constitution, which in his view forbade the exercise by the General Government of anything but expressly delegated powers. It would have seemed like a contradiction in terms to expect either of these statesmen to agree upon a proposition which radically contravened the inmost convictions of each of them. But the nature of things was more powerful than either a Bonaparte or a

Jefferson. No human influence could have controlled either of them, but the stars in their courses were still stronger, and they gladly obeyed the mandate of fate, which was in each case the mandate of an enlightened patriotism. France, divesting herself of this rich incumbrance, was the better fitted for the supreme gladiatorial effort that awaited her, and Jefferson gained an immortal fame by preferring an immense benefit to his country to consistency in a narrow construction of the written law.

No man, no party, can fight with any chance of final success against a cosmic tendency; no cleverness, no popularity, avails against the spirit of the age. In obeying that invincible tendency, against all his political convictions, Jefferson secured a conspicuous place in history; while the Federalist politicians who should have welcomed this signal illustration and proof of the truth of their theory of the power of the Government they had framed, through the influence of party spirit faltered in their faith and brought upon their party a lasting eclipse through their failure to discern the signs of the times. President Roosevelt, in the memorable address with which he dedicated last year this exhibition, used, in relation to this subject, these striking words: "As is so often the case in nature, the law of development of a living organism showed itself in its actual workings to be wiser than the wisdom of the wisest."

A glance at the map of Europe gives an idea of the vastness of this acquisition. It covers a space greater that that occupied by France, Germany, Great Britain, Italy, Spain, and Portugal; it overlaps the familiar world of history and literature. In its ample field grew up fourteen of our Commonwealths; a taxable wealth of seven thousand millions of dollars accumulated there and a population of sixteen million souls have there found their home, drawn not only from our elder communities, but from the teeming hives of humanity—the officinæ gentium—in every land beneath the quickening sun.

But more important than the immense material increase in the extent and resources of the new Republic was this establishment of the principle, thus early in its career, that it was to assume no inferior position to other nations in its power to acquire territory, to extend its influence—in short, to do all that any independent, self-respecting power might do which was in accord with public morals, conducive to the general welfare, and not prohibited by the Constitution. Though the Federalists failed to embrace this great opportunity and thereby brought upon their party an Iliad of woes, the precedent had been set for all time for their successors. The nation had outgrown its swaddling clothes. Even the most impassioned advocates of strict construction felt this time that it was the letter that killeth and the spirit that giveth life. The nation moved on its imperial course. The new chart and compass were in our hands. The national principle once established, other things were naturally added unto us. Lewis and Clarke, following and illustrating the great law of westerly migration, pushed through the wilderness and planted our banners by the shores of the Peaceful Sea. In the process of years Texas and the wide expanse of New Mexico came to us, and California, bringing a dower of the countless riches that for unknown ages had veined her hills. Even the shores of the ocean could not long check the Eagle in his marvelous flight. The isles of the uttermost seas became his stepping-stones.

This, gentlemen, is the lesson which we are called to contemplate amid the courts and the palaces of this universal exhibition; that when a nation exists, founded in righteousness and justice, whose object and purposes are the welfare of humanity, the things which make for its growth and the increase of its power, so long as it is true to its ideals, are sure to come to pass, no matter what political theories or individual sentiments stand in the way. The common good will ultimately prevail, though it "mock the counsels of the wise and the valor of the brave." I know what snares may lie in this idea—how it may serve as the cry of demagogues and the pretext for despots. Woe be unto the nation which misuses it! but shame and disaster is also the portion of those who fear to follow its luminous beaconing.

From every part of the world you have gathered to share in this secular festival of historic memories. You represent not only the world-wide community of intelligence, but the wonderful growth in these modern days of universal sympathy and good will—what our poet Bayard Taylor, speaking on a similar occasion in Vienna, and adding, I believe, a new word to the German language, called Weltgemuethlichkeit. Of all the phenomena of the last hundred years there is none more wonderful than that increase of mutual knowledge which has led inevitably to a corresponding increase in mutual toleration and esteem. The credit of this great advance in civilization belongs to the press of the world. It is true that it is the modest boast of modern diplomacy that its office is the removal of misunderstandings—that, so far as intentions go, its ways are pleasantness and its paths are peace; but how slight are the results that the best-intentioned diplomat can attain in this direction, compared with the illuminating blaze of light which the press each morning radiates on the universe! We can not claim that the light is all of one color, nor that there are not many angles of refraction; but, from this endless variety of opinion and assertion, truth at last emerges, and every day adds something to the world's knowledge of itself. There is a wise French proverb, "to understand is to pardon," and every step of progress which the peoples of the earth make in their comprehension of each other's conditions and motives is a step forward in the march to the goal desired by men and angels, of universal peace and brotherhood.

Upon none of the arts or professions has the tremendous acceleration of progress in recent years had more effect than upon that of which you are the representatives. We easily grow used to miracles; it will seem a mere commonplace when I say that all the wonders of the magicians invented by those ingenious oriental poets who wrote the Arabian Nights, pale before the stupendous facts which you handle in your daily lives. The air has scarcely ceased to vibrate with the utterances of kings and rulers in the older realms, when their words are read in the streets of St. Louis and on the farms of Nebraska. The telegraph is too quick for the calendar; you may read in your evening paper a dispatch from the antipodes with a date of the following day. The details of a battle on the shores of the Hermit Kingdom—a land which a few years ago was hidden in the mists of legend—are printed and commented on before the blood of the wounded has ceased to flow. Almost before the smoke of the conflict has lifted we read the obituaries of the unsepultured dead. And not only do you record with the swiftness of thought these incidents of war and violence, but the daily victories of truth over error, of light over darkness; the spread of commerce in distant seas, the inventions of industry, the discoveries of science, are all placed instantly within the knowledge of millions. The seeds of thought, perfected in one climate, blossom and fructify under every sky, in every nationality which the sun visits.

With these miraculous facilities, with this unlimited power, comes also an enormous responsibility in the face of God and man. I am not here to preach to you a gospel whose lessons are known to you far better than to me. I am not calling sinners to repentance, but I am following a good tradition in stirring up the pure minds of the righteous by way of remembrance. It is well for us to reflect on the vast import, the endless chain of results, of that globe-encircling speech you address each day to the world. Your winged words have no fixed flight; like the lightning, they traverse the ether according to laws of their own. They light in every clime; they influence a thousand different varieties of minds and manners. How vastly important is it, then, that the sentiments they convey should be those of good will rather than of malevolence, those of national concord rather than of prejudice, those of peace rather than of hostility. The temptation to the contrary is almost irresistible. I acknowledge with contrition how often I have fallen by the way. It is far more amusing to attack than to defend, to excite than to soothe. But the highest victory of great power is that of self-restraint, and it would be a beneficent result of this memorable meeting, this œcumenical council of the press, if it taught us all—the brethren of this mighty priesthood—that mutual knowledge of each other which should modify prejudices, restrain acerbity of thought and expression, and tend in some degree to bring in that blessed time

> When light shall spread, and man be liker man
> Through all the seasons of the Golden Year.

What better school was ever seen in which to learn the lesson of mutual esteem and forbearance, than this great exposition? The nations of the earth are met here in friendly competition. The first thing that strikes the visitor is the infinite diversity of thought and effort which characterizes the several exhibits; but a closer study every day reveals a resemblance of mind and purpose more marvelous still. Integrity, industry, the intelligent adaptation of means to ends, are everywhere the indispensable conditions of success. Honest work, honest dealing, these qualities mark the winner in every part of the world. The artist, the poet, the artisan, and the statesman, they everywhere stand or fall through the lack or the possession of similar qualities. How shall one people hate or despise another when we have seen how like us they are in most respects, and how superior they are in some! Why should we not revert to the ancient wisdom which regarded nothing human as alien, and to the words of Holy Writ which remind us that the Almighty has made all men brethren?

In the name of the President—writer,

soldier, and statesman, eminent in all three professions and in all equally an advocate of justice, peace, and good will,—I bid you a cordial welcome, with the prayer that this meeting of the representatives of the world's intelligence may be fruitful in advantage to the press of all nations, and may bring us somewhat nearer to the dawn of the day of peace on earth and good will among men. Let us remember that we are met to celebrate the transfer of a vast empire from one nation to another without the firing of a shot, without the shedding of one drop of blood. If the press of the world would adopt and persist in the high resolve that war should be no more, the clangor of arms would cease from the rising of the sun to its going down, and we could fancy that at last our ears, no longer stunned by the din of armies, might hear the morning stars singing together and all the sons of God shouting for joy.

FIFTY YEARS OF THE REPUBLICAN PARTY

JACKSON, MICHIGAN, JULY 6th, 1904

FIFTY YEARS OF THE REPUBLICAN PARTY

A CENTURY is but a moment of history; it has often happened that several of them have passed away, since men began to record their deeds, with little change in the physical aspect or the moral progress of the world. But at other times—of intense action and spiritual awakening—a single generation may form an epoch; and few periods of equal duration in political annals have been so crowded with great events as the fifty years we celebrate to-day. Under the oaks of Jackson, on the 6th of July, 1854, a party was brought into being and baptized, which ever since has answered the purposes of its existence with fewer follies and failures and more magnificent achievements than ordinarily fall to the lot of any institution of mortal origin. And even the beginning of the end is not yet. This historic party is only now in the full maturity of its power and its capacity for good. We look back upon a past of unparalleled usefulness and glory with emotions of thankfulness and pride; we confront the future and its exacting problems with a confidence born of the experience of difficulties surmounted and triumphs achieved in paths more thorny and ways more arduous than any that are likely to challenge the courage and the conscience of the generation which is to follow us. It is meet that at this stage of our journey we should review the past and read its lessons, and in its light take heart for what lies beyond.

The Republican party had a noble origin. It sprang directly from an aroused and indignant national conscience. Questions of finance, of political economy, of orderly administration, passed out of sight for the moment, to be taken up and dealt with later on. But in 1854 the question that brought the thinking men together was whether there should be a limit to the aggressions of slavery; and in 1861 that solemn inquiry turned to one still more portentous, Should the nation live or die? The humblest old Republican in America has the right to be proud that in the days of his youth in the presence of these momentous questions he judged right; and if he is sleeping in his honored grave his children may justly be glad of his decision.

It was not so easy fifty years ago to take sides against the slave power as it may seem to-day. Respect for the vested rights of the Southern people was one of our most sacred traditions. It was founded on the compromises of the Constitution, and upon a long line of legal and legislative precedents. The men of the Revolution made no defense of slavery in itself; Washington, Adams, Jefferson, and Franklin deplored its existence, but recognized the necessity of compromise until the public mind might rest in the hope of its ultimate extinction. But after they had passed away, improvements in the culture and manufacture of cotton made this uneconomic form of labor for the time profitable, and what had been merely tolerated as a temporary necessity began to be upheld as a permanent system. Slavery entrenched itself in every department of our public life. Its advocates dominated Congress and the State legislatures; they even invaded the pulpit and grotesquely wrested a few texts of scripture to their purpose. They gave the tone to society; even the Southern accent was imitated in our schools and colleges.

If the slaveholders had been content with their unquestioned predominance, they might for many years have controlled our political and social world. It was natural for the conservative people of the North to say: "We deplore the existence of slavery, but we are all to blame for it; we should not cast upon our brethren in the South the burdens and perils of its abolition. We must bear with the unfortunate condition of things and take our share of its inconveniences." But the slaveholding party could not rest content. The ancients said that madness was the fate of those judged by the gods. Continual aggression is a necessity of a false position. They felt instinctively that if their system were permanently to endure it must be extended, and to attain this object they were ready to risk everything. They rent in twain the compromises which had protected them so long. They tore down the bulwarks which had at once restricted and defended them; and confiding in their strength and our patience, they boldly announced and inaugurated the policy of the indefinite extension of their "peculiar institution."

Once embarked upon this fatal enterprise they left nothing undone which could contribute to the catastrophe upon which they were rushing. The Whig party had gone to ruin in 1852 on account of the impossibility of combining the scattered elements of opposition to the party of pro-slavery aggression; but they themselves furnished the weapon which was to defeat them. In May, 1854, after several months of passionate debate, to which the country listened with feverish interest, Congress passed the bill organizing the Territories of Kansas and Nebraska, omitting the restrictions of the Missouri Compromise which excluded slavery from them. This action at once precipitated the floating anti-slavery sentiment of the country. A mighty cry of resolute indignation arose from one end of the land to the other. The hollow truce, founded upon the legitimate compromises which had been observed in good faith by one side and ruthlessly violated by the other, was at an end. Men began to search their consciences instead of the arguments of political expediency. A discussion of the right and wrong of slavery became general; the light was let in, fatal to darkness. A system which degraded men, dishonored women, deprived little children of the sacred solace of home, was doomed from the hour it passed into the arena of free debate. And even if we shut our eyes to the moral aspects of that heartless system, and confined ourselves to the examination of its economic merits, it was found to be wasteful and inefficient. The Americans are at once the most sentimental and the most practical of peoples—and when they see that an institution is morally revolting, and, besides, does not pay, its fate is sealed.

Yet the most wonderful feature of that extraordinary campaign which then began, and which never ceased until the land was purged of its deadly sin, was that even in the very "tempest and whirlwind of their passion" the great leaders of the Republican party kept their agitation strictly within the limits of the Constitution and the law. There was no general demand for even an amendment to the organic instrument. They pleaded for the repeal of unjust statutes as inconsistent with the Constitution, but did not advocate their violation. Only among the more obscure and ardent members of the party was there any demand for the abolition of slavery, but the whole party stood like a rock for the principle that the damnable institution must be content with what it had already got, and must not be allowed to pollute another inch of free soil. On this impregnable ground they made their stand; and the mass convention which assembled here in 1854, while the vibrations of the thunder of the guns and the shoutings of the birthday of Liberty yet lingered in the air, gave a nucleus and a name to the new party, destined to a great and beneficent career. Before the month ended, the anti-slavery men of five more great States adopted the name "Republican," and under that banner Congress was carried and two years later a national party assembled at Pittsburg and nominated Fremont and Dayton, who failed by a few votes of sweeping the North.

Who of us that was living then will ever forget the ardent enthusiasm of those days? It was one of those periods, rare in the life of any nation, when men forget themselves and, in spite of habit, of interest, and of prejudice, follow their consciences wherever they may lead. In the clear, keen air that was abroad, the best men in the country drew deeper breaths and rose to a moral height they had not before attained. The movement was universal. Sumner in the East, Seward in New York, Chase in Ohio, Bates in Missouri, Blair in Maryland, all sent forth their identical appeal to the higher motive; and in Illinois, where the most popular man in the State boldly and cynically announced, "I don't care whether slavery is voted up or voted down," a voice, new to the nation, replied, "There are some of us who *do* care. If slavery is not wrong, nothing is wrong"—and Abraham Lincoln came upon the field not to leave it until he was triumphant in death.

I have no right to detain you at this hour in recounting the history of those memorable days. Two incidents of the long battle will never be forgotten. One was the physical and political contest for the possession of Kansas, carried on with desperate courage and recklessness of consequences by the pro-slavery party on the one side, and, on the other, by the

New England farmers whose weapons of aggression were Bible texts and the words of Jefferson, and whose arms of defense were Sharpe's rifles. With words that ring even now when we read them, like the clashing of swords, the Slave State men claimed Kansas as their right and the Free State men replied in the words of the prophet before Herod, It is not lawful for you to have her. And when the talking sharpened to the physical clinch, the praying men fought with the same ferocity as the men who cursed. In the field of political discussion the most dramatic incident of the fight was the debate between Lincoln and Douglas. Not many of you saw that battle of the strong, where each of the gladiators had an adversary worthy of his steel, where the audiences were equally divided, where the combatants were fairly matched in debating skill and address, and where the superiority of Lincoln was not so much personal as it was in the overwhelming strength of his position. He was fighting for freedom and could say so; Douglas was fighting for slavery and could not avow it. The result of the contest is now seen to have been inevitable. Douglas was reëlected to the Senate but had gained also the resentful suspicion of the South, which two years later disowned him and defeated his lifelong ambition. Lincoln became at once the foremost Republican of the West and a little later the greatest political figure of the century.

If there is one thing more than another in which we Republicans are entitled to a legitimate pride, it is that Lincoln was our first President; that we believed in him, loyally supported him while he lived, and that we have never lost the right to call ourselves his followers. There is not a principle avowed by the Republican party to-day which is out of harmony with his teachings or inconsistent with his character. We do not object to our opponents quoting him, praising him—even claiming him as their own. If it is not sincere, it is still a laudable tribute to acknowledged excellence. If it is genuine, it is still better, for even a Nebraska Populist who reads his Lincoln is in the way of salvation. But only those who believe in human rights and are willing to make sacrifices to defend them; who believe in the nation and its beneficent power; who believe in the American system of protection championed by a long line of our greatest and best, running back from McKinley to Washington, and, as Senator Dolliver so truthfully said, "to the original sources of American common sense"; only those who believe in equal justice to labor and to capital; in honest money and the right to earn it, have any title to name themselves by the name of Lincoln, or to claim a moral kinship with that august and venerated spirit. I admit it would be little less than sacrilege to try to trade upon that benignant Renown, whose light "folds in this orb o' the earth." But we who have always tried to walk in the road he pointed out can not be deprived of the tender pride of calling ourselves his disciples, and of doing in his name the work allotted to us by Providence. And I hope I am violating neither the confidence of a friend nor the proprieties of an occasion like this when I refer to the ardent and able young statesman who is now, and is to be, our President, to let you know that in times of doubt and difficulty the thought oftenest in his heart is, "What, in such a case, would Lincoln have done?"

As we are removed further and further from

the founders of our party and their mighty work, their names and their fame rise every year higher in the great perspective of history. The clamor of hatred and calumny dies away. The efforts made to weaken the hands of Lincoln and his associates are forgotten. The survivors of those who so bitterly attacked him and his cause, which was the cause of the country, are now themselves astonished when confronted with the words they then uttered. But it was against a political opposition not less formidable and efficient than the armed force beyond the Potomac that the Union men of that day, and their President, had to struggle. It was not merely the losses in battle, the waste of our wealth, the precious blood of our young men, that filled Lincoln's heart with anguish and made him old before his time, but it was the storm of partisan hostility that raged against him, filling the air with slanders and thwarting his most earnest and unselfish efforts for the country's good. But in spite of it all he persevered, never for a moment tempted by the vast power he wielded to any action not justified by the moral and the organic law. I have always liked the inscription on the medal which the workmen of France, by one-cent subscriptions, caused to be struck after his death: "Abraham Lincoln, the honest man. Waged war. Abolished slavery. Twice elected President without veiling the face of Liberty." This was an achievement new to the world: that a man and a party, armed with an authority so unquestioned and so stupendous, in the very current of a vast war, should have submitted themselves so rigidly to the law—and never have dreamed there was anything meritorious about it. Then, if never before, we proved we were as fit to be free as the men who achieved our freedom.

The world learned other lessons in swift succession. We disbanded our army—sent them home to earn their livings as simple citizens of the land they had saved, without terms or conditions: they asked none; they wanted peace; they were glad to get to work. And there were no reprisals, not a man punished for rebellion or treason; not an act of violence sullied the glory of victory. The fight had been fierce, but loyal; we at least wished the reconciliation to be perfect. Then came the paying of our debts. To whom is the credit due of that enormous task, that sublime effort of common honesty, if not to the party which against every assault of open and covert repudiation stood by the country's honor and kept it free from stain?

Let me hurriedly enumerate a few of the events in the long and fruitful career of the Republican party which seem to us to entitle it to the confidence of the country and the final approval of history. After the war was ended and peace reëstablished with no damage to the structure of the Government, but, on the contrary, with added strength and with increased guaranties of its perpetuity, it remained to be shown whether the power and success of the Republican party were to be permanent, or whether, born of a crisis, it was fitted to cope with the problems of daily national life. It had destroyed slavery, or, perhaps we might better say, it had created the conditions by which slavery had committed suicide. In the absence of this great adversary, could the party hold together against the thousand lesser evils that beset the public life of modern peoples—the evils of ignorance, corruption, avarice, and lawlessness, the prejudices of race and of class, the voices of demagogues, the cunning of dishonest craft, the brutal tyranny of the boss, the venality of the mean? I think it is not too much to say that the last forty years have given an answer, full of glory and honor, to that question. The Republican party, in the mass and in detail, has shown its capacity to govern. By the homestead law, with equal generosity and wisdom, it distributed the immense national domain among the citizens who were willing to cultivate it and who have converted wide stretches of wilderness into smiling homes. It built the Pacific Railroad, which has bound the Union together from East to West by bands of steel and made the States beyond the mountains among our most loyal and prosperous commonwealths. It redeemed our paper currency and made all our forms of money of exactly equal value, and our credit the best in the world. By persistent honesty in our finances—in the face of obstacles which might have daunted the hardiest statesmen—it has reduced our interest charges so that in any mart on earth we can borrow money cheaper than any other people. In the financial revulsions to which all communities are subject, we are able, thanks to our laws and our administrative system, to meet and pass the most violent crises without lasting damage to our prosperity. We have, by the patient labor of years, so succeeded in reforming and regulating our civil service that patronage has almost ceased to cast its deadly blight upon the work of our public servants. Human nature is weak and offenses happen; but they are almost always found out and are punished without mercy when detected. By persistent adherence to the policy of protection, we have given to our industries a development which the fathers of the Republic never dreamed of; which, besides supplying our home market, has carried our manufactures to the uttermost ends of the earth.

History affords no parallel to the vast and increasing prosperity which this country has enjoyed under Republican rule. I hasten to say we do not claim to have invented seedtime and harvest, and industry and thrift. We are a great people and success is our right; God is good to those who behave themselves. But we may justly claim that the Republican party has been in power during these years of marvelous growth, and we can at least bring proof that we have not prevented it—and this is no slight honor for a party to claim. I will not at this moment speak of the important acquisitions of territory we have made, which render us in many ways the predominant power in the Pacific. But out of the territory we already possessed, fourteen new States have entered the Union. The census of 1850 gave us 23,000,000 of population—the last one, 76,000,000. The number of our farms—the total of our cultivated acreage—has increased fourfold. Our corn crop is five times what it was; our wheat crop, six times. The capital invested in manufacturing has grown from five hundred millions to ten billions; where it employed less than a million artisans, it now employs more than five millions; and while the number of workingmen has increased five times, their wages have increased tenfold. The value of manufactured property is thirteen times what it was when the Republicans of Michigan met under the oaks. The real and personal wealth of the country has grown in this amazing half century from seven thousand millions to ninety-four thousand millions. Our railroads have grown from a mileage of 16,000 to one of 200,000. Our imports and exports have gone up by leaps and bounds to the same monstrous proportions. And finally, let us hasten to say, as the other side will say it for us, instead of the $47,000,000 which supplied our modest needs in 1850 we now collect and spend some $700,000,000 annually. I can only add what Speaker Reed replied to a Democratic statesman who complained of a billion-dollar Congress: "Well! this is a billion-dollar country."

Of course our opponents, who have got far enough from the men and the events of the great war period to admit they were not without merit, will say—for they must say something—that we have fallen away from that high level. Now, I am grieved to confess that I am old enough to have seen something of the beginning, as well as of the present, of Republican Administrations, and I venture to say that no eight years of government in our history have been purer from blame or have conferred greater benefits upon the country than the eight years of McKinley and Roosevelt which claim your approval to-day. I need not hesitate to refer to it, although I have been associated with both Administrations; so little of their merit is mine that I may speak of them without false modesty. Our national finances have never in our history been so wisely and successfully administered; our credit never stood on a basis so broad and so strong. Our two-percents command a premium in all markets—no other country on earth can say as much. We paid abroad the other day fifty millions of gold in a single transaction without producing a ripple in exchange. The vast expenditure made necessary by our enormous increase in every element of national growth is collected with the utmost ease and expended with perfect honesty. Our protective system, loyally and intelligently carried out and improved in the last seven years, not only fills our Treasury with the means of national expenditure, but has carried our industries and our commerce to a height of prosperity which is the wonder and envy of our neighbors, who are trying to emulate our progress. In the relations between labor and capital, always a subject of deep concern in democratic governments, we have improved both in the letter and the spirit. How could it be otherwise when labor knows that McKinley and Roosevelt have watched over its interests as a brother might, and capital knows that its rights will be sacredly guarded so long as it is true to its duties?

As to our place in the world it has simply followed and naturally complemented the steady improvement in our domestic condition. A country growing so fast must have elbowroom—must have its share of the sunshine. In the last seven years, without aggression, without undue self-assertion, we have taken the place that belongs to us. Adhering with religious care to the precepts of Washington and the traditions of a century, and avoiding all entangling alliances, professing friendship to all nations and partiality to none, McKinley and Roosevelt have gone steadily forward protecting and extending American interests everywhere and gaining, by deserving it, the good will of all the world. Their advice has been constantly sought and sparingly given. By constant iteration their policy has been made plain. We do not covet the territory nor the control of any other people. We hold ourselves absolutely apart from any combinations or groups of powers. We favor no national interests but our own. In controversies among our neighbors we take no part, not even tendering good offices unless at the request of both parties concerned. When our advice is given, it is always on the side of peace and conciliation. We have made, it is true, great acquisitions, but never of set purpose nor from greed of land. In the case of Hawaii, the will of the people of those islands coincided with the important interests we have to guard in the Pacific. In the Samoan treaty we freed ourselves from a useless and dangerous entanglement, and in place of an undesirable condominium we gained possession of the best harbor in the South Seas, retaining, at the same time, all our commercial rights in the archipelago. The diplomacy of McKinley and Roosevelt has been directed principally to our present and future interests in the Pacific, on whose wide shores so much of the world's work is to be done. They have constantly kept in view the vast importance of that opening field of our activities. The long negotiations for the "open door" in China; the steadfast fight we made for the integrity of that ancient Empire; President McKinley's attitude throughout the Boxer troubles, so severely criticized at the time and so splendidly approved by the results; the position President Roosevelt has since held and now holds in regard to the neutrality of China in the present war—have all been dictated by one consistent policy, of taking care that our interests receive no detriment in the Pacific; that while we wish no harm to anyone else, we shall see that no damage is done to our people, no door is shut in our face.

The negotiations begun by McKinley and successfully completed by Roosevelt for the abrogation of the Clayton-Bulwer Treaty, which impeded our freedom of action in building an Isthmian canal, was a part of the same general plan of opening a field of enterprise in those distant regions where the Far West becomes the Far East. In this matter we were met in the most frank and friendly spirit by the British Government, as also in the matter of the Alaskan boundary, which was settled for all time by a high judicial tribunal removing a cloud upon our title to another great Pacific possession. And to close this record of success—monotonous because gained by appeals to reason rather than force, without parade or melodrama—came the treaty with Panama, by which we finally gained the pathway across the Isthmus by a perpetual grant, ensuring the construction of an American canal under American control, built primarily for American needs, but open on equal terms to all the people of good will the world over.

All the foreign policy of McKinley and Roosevelt has been marked with the same stamp of honesty and fair dealing, confessedly in American interests, but treating our friends with equity and consideration. They have made more treaties than any two preceding Presidents; and the conclusion of the whole matter is that we stand to-day in independent though amicable relations to all the rest of the world—without an ally and without an enemy.

If the Government for the last seven years had done nothing else, it would have entitled itself to an honorable place in history by the manner in which it has handled the questions of the islands whose destiny has been so interwoven with our own. The war with Spain was carried through with incredible swiftness and energy, without a shadow of corruption, without a moral or a technical fault. A hundred days sufficed for the fighting. Diplomacy then did its work, and our commissioners brought home a treaty so just and so beneficial that it was impossible to unite the opposition against it. Then came the far more difficult and delicate task of administration. You remember the doleful prophecies of evil with which the air was filled; that we had not the habit nor the ability to govern outlying possessions; that the islands would be cesspools of jobbery and fraud; that the enterprise was conceived in violence and would go out in disaster. And now you know the result. The Republic never is in default of men to serve it worthily when the Chief of the State is honest and able; when he has the eye and the will to choose the best men and will be satisfied with no less. So in Cuba, Porto Rico, and the Philippines we got the best we had. Wood, Allen and Hunt, and Taft have each in his place wrought a great work and gained a righteous fame. Cuba and Porto Rico are free and enjoying—the one under her own banner, the other under the Stars and Stripes—a degree of prosperity and happiness never known before in all their troubled story.

As to the Philippines, the work done there by Judge Taft and his associates will rank among the highest achievements of colonial administration recorded in history. Never since their discovery has there been such general peace and order; so thorough a protection of the peaceable and restraint of evil doers; so wide a diffusion of education; so complete a guaranty to industry of the fruit of its labors. And when they see this energetic and efficient government carried on, free from the venality and bribery which formerly seemed to them a necessity of existence, then, indeed, they are like them that dream. The principal evil from which they still suffer has its origin here. Some well-meaning people—and others not so well meaning—are constantly persuading them that they are oppressed and that they will be given their liberty, as they choose to call it, as soon as the Republican party is overthrown in this country. These are the true enemies of the Filipinos, and not the men who are striving with whole-hearted energy and with consummate success to ameliorate their condition and to make them fit for self-government and all its attendant advantages. The so-called anti-imperialists confound in their daily speeches and writings two absolutely unrelated ideas—the liberty, the civil rights, the self-government which we have given the Filipinos, and the independence which the best of them do not want and know they are unable to maintain. To abandon them now, to cast them adrift at the mercy of accident, would be an act of cowardice and treachery which would gain us the scorn and reproach of civilization.

Our opponents sometimes say we have no right to claim the credit of the great deeds of the last half-century—that we could not have accomplished them without the aid of Democrats. Nothing truer was ever said; and it is one of the chief glories of our annals, and it forms the surest foundation of our hopes for the future. The principles upon which our party is built are so sound, they have so irresistible an attraction to patriotic and fair-minded men, that whenever a time of crisis comes, when the national welfare is clearly at stake, when voters must decide whether they shall follow their prejudices or their consciences, we draw from other parties their best men by thousands. Bright among the brightest of those who founded our party shine the names of Democrats; and when the war came on, the picked men of that party rallied to the colors. Douglas, shortly before he died, declared his unfaltering support of Lincoln. The sun would go down before I could name the Democrats who fought like heroes for the country. Grant, Sherman, Sheridan, Dix, Sickles, Logan—in short, an innumerable host, Democrats all, rushed into the field and thereafter fought and worked with the Republicans while life lasted. And that vast majority of Lincoln's in 1864 would have been impossible had not myriads of Democrats, casting their life-long associations to the winds, listened to the inward monitor which said, "Choose you this day whom ye will serve."

As it was then, so it has been in after years. When the attempt was made to repudiate, in whole or in part, the national debt; or to abolish the system of protection to American industries, founded by Washington and Hamilton, and approved by the experience of a hundred years; or to degrade our currency at the demand of mere ignorance and greed—in all these cases we saw the proof of the homely adage that you may lead a horse to the water but cannot make him drink. In spite of organizations and platforms, in spite of the frantic adjurations of gifted orators, hosts of patriotic Democrats walked quietly to the polls and voted as their consciences dictated, in the interests of the public welfare rather than of a party. Even in so lofty and restricted an arena as our Senate, we have seen the ablest and most adroit organizer of his party fail in the most energetic effort of his life to induce his party to reject a great national benefit because it was offered by Republican hands. Half the Democratic Senators said this was no question for pettifogging politics and voted for an American canal across the Isthmus.

We are not claiming that we monopolize the virtue or the patriotism of the country. There are good men in all parties. I know far better men than I am who are Democrats. But we are surely allowed, in a love feast like this, to talk of what has been done by the family, and at least to brag a little of the Democrats who have helped us. We get their votes for one reason only—because we started right and in the main have kept right. We invite accessions from the ranks of our patriotic opponents, and we shall get them in the future, as we have in the past, whenever we deserve them. We shall get them this year, because this year we do deserve them. We come before the country in a position which cannot be successfully attacked in front, or flank, or rear. What we have done, what we are doing, and what we intend to do—on all three we confidently challenge the verdict of the American people. The record of fifty years will show whether as a party we are fit to govern; the state of our domestic and foreign affairs will show whether as a party we have fallen off; and both together will show whether we can be trusted for a while longer.

Our platform is before the country. Perhaps it is lacking in novelty. There is certainly nothing sensational about it. It is substantially the platform on which we won two great victories in the name of McKinley, and it is still sound and serviceable. Its principles have been tested by eight years of splendid success and have received the approval of the country. It is in line with all our platforms of the past, except where prophecy and promise in those days have become history in these. We stand by the ancient ways which have proved good.

It would take a wizard to guess what a dainty dish our adversaries will set before the sovereign people to-morrow. Their State conventions have given them a rich variety to choose from. As to money, they range all the way from Bedlam to Belmont; as to tariff, the one wing in Maryland is almost sane, the other wants raving free trade and dynamite for the custom-houses. When they discuss our island possessions, some want to scuttle away and abandon them out of hand; others agree with that sensible Southerner who said: "What 's the use talking about expansion. Great Scott! we 've done expanded!" One thing is reasonably sure: they will get as near to our platform as they possibly can and they will by implication approve everything McKinley and Roosevelt have done in the last four years. They will favor sound finance and a tariff which will not disturb business; rigid honesty in administration and prompt punishment of the dishonest; the Monroe Doctrine and an Isthmian canal. To be logical they ought to go on and nominate the Republican candidates who are pledged to all these laudable policies.

But they will not be logical. They do not care to oppose our policy; they merely deny our sincerity in avowing it. They cannot deny the soundness of our principles; they pretend themselves to hold them. But the function of an opposition is to oppose, and as they are otherwise destitute of an issue they seek to make a few by attributing to us principles we have never dreamed of holding and policies which are abhorrent to us. And distrusting the effect of these maneuvers in advance, they announce their plan of campaign to be not pro-anything, but anti-Roosevelt. This is a mere counsel of desperation, and the Republicans will gladly accept the issue.

Even on this narrow issue they will dodge most of the details. Ask them, Has the President been a good citizen, a good soldier, a good man in all personal relations? Is he a man of intelligence, of education? Does he know this country well? Does he know the world outside? Has he studied law, history, and politics? Has he had great chances to learn, and has he improved them? Is he sound and strong in mind, body, and soul? Is he accessible and friendly to all sorts and conditions of men? Has he the courage and the candor, and the God-given ability to speak to the people and tell them what he thinks? To all these questions they will answer, Yes. Then what is your objection to him? They will either stand speechless or they will answer with the parrot cry which we have heard so often: He is unsafe!

In a certain sense we shall have to admit this to be true. To every grade of lawbreaker, high or low; to a man who would rob a till or a ballot box; to the sneak or the bully; to the hypocrite and the humbug, Theodore Roosevelt is more than unsafe; he is positively dangerous.

But let us be serious with these good people. What are the coefficients of safety in a Chief of State? He should have courage; the wisest coward that ever lived is not fit to rule. And intelligence; we want no blunder-headed hero in the White House. And honesty; a clever thief would do infinite mischief. These three are the indispensables. With them a man is all the more safe if he has a sense of proportion, a sense of humor, a wide knowledge of men and affairs; if he seeks good counsel; and, finally, if he is a patriot, if he loves his country, believes in it, and seeks in all things its interest and its glory. Any man may make mistakes; but such a man as this will make few, and no grave ones.

Such a man is our President and our candidate. He is prompt and energetic, but he takes infinite pains to get at the facts before he acts. In all the crises in which he has been accused of undue haste, his action has been the result of long meditation and well-reasoned conviction. If he think rapidly, that is no fault; he thinks thoroughly, and that is the essential. When he made peace between the miners and the operators, it was no sudden caprice but the fruit of serious reflection, and this act of mingled philanthropy and common sense was justified by a great practical result. When he proclaimed anew the Monroe Doctrine in the Venezuela case his action was followed by the most explicit acceptance of that saving policy which has ever come to us from overseas. He acted very swiftly, it is true, in Mississippi, when the best citizens of a town threatened the life of a postmistress for no fault but her color. He simply said, "Very well, gentlemen; you may get your letters somewhere else for a while."

And as to the merger suits, now that people have come to their senses they see that his action in that case was as regular as the equinox. He was informed through legal channels that a statute had been violated. He did not make the statute, but he was bound by his oath to execute it. He brought the proceeding which it was his duty to bring. The courts, from the lowest to the highest, sustained his action. He did what it would have been a high misdemeanor not to have done. The laws in this country are made to be obeyed, whether it is safe or not. It is always unsafe to disobey them.

But there has been more noise made over his suddenness on the Isthmus of Panama than elsewhere. It is difficult to treat this charge with seriousness. The President had made a treaty with Colombia at her own solicitation, which was infinitely to her advantage, to inaugurate an enterprise which was to be for the benefit of the world. He waited with endless patience while Bogotá delayed and trifled with the matter, and finally rejected it, and suggested new negotiations for a larger sum. Panama, outraged by this climax of the wrongs she had already suffered, declared and established her independence. The President, following an unbroken line of precedents, entered into relations with the new Republic, and, obeying his duty to protect the transit of the Isthmus as all other Presidents had done before him, gave orders that there should be no bloodshed on the line of the railway. He said, like Grant, "Let us have peace," and we had it. It will seem incredible to posterity that any American could have objected to this. He acted wisely and beneficently, and all some people can find to criticise in his action is that he was too brisk about it. If a thing is right and proper to do, it does not make it criminal to do it promptly. No, gentlemen! That was a time when the hour and the man arrived together. He struck while the iron was white hot on the anvil of opportunity, and forged as perfect a bit of honest statecraft as this generation has seen.

We could desire no better fortune, in the campaign upon which we are entering, than that the other side should persist in their announced intention to make the issue upon President Roosevelt. What a godsend to our orators! It takes some study, some research, to talk about the tariff, or the currency, or foreign policy. But to talk about Roosevelt! it is as easy as to sing "the glory of the Graeme." Of gentle birth and breeding, yet a man of the people in the best sense; with the training of a scholar and the breezy accessibility of a ranchman; a man of the library and a man of the world; an athlete and a thinker; a soldier and a statesman; a reader, a writer, and a maker of history; with the sensibility of a poet and the steel nerve of a rough rider; one who never did, and never could, turn his back on a friend or an enemy. A man whose merits are so great that he could win on his merits alone; whose personality is so engaging that you lose sight of his merits. Make their fight on a man like that! What irreverent caricaturist was it that called them the Stupid party?

In our candidate for the Vice-Presidency we have followed the old and commendable custom of the Republic, and have nominated a man in every way fit for the highest place in the nation, who will bring to the Presidency of the Senate an ability and experience rarely equaled in its history.

I have detained you too long; yet as I close I want to say a word to the young men whose political life is beginning. Anyone entering business would be glad of the chance to become one of an established firm with years of success behind it, with a wide connection, with unblemished character, with credit founded on a rock. How infinitely brighter the future when the present is so sure, the past so glorious. Everything great done by this country in the last fifty years has been done under the auspices of the Republican party. Is not this consciousness a great asset to have in your mind and memory? As a mere item of personal comfort is it not worth having? Lincoln and Grant, Hayes and Garfield, Harrison and McKinley —names secure in the heaven of fame,—they all are gone, leaving small estates in worldly goods, but what vast possessions in principles, memories, sacred associations! It is a start in life to share that wealth. Who now boasts that he opposed Lincoln? who brags of his voting against Grant? though both acts may have been from the best of motives. In our form of government there must be two parties, and tradition, circumstances, temperament, will always create a sufficient opposition. But what young man would not rather belong to the party that does things, instead of one that opposes them; to the party that looks up, rather than down; to the party of the dawn, rather than of the sunset. For fifty years the Republican party has believed in the country and labored for it in hope and joy; it has reverenced the flag and followed it; has carried it under strange skies and planted it on far-receding horizons. It has seen the nation grow greater every year and more respected; by just dealing, by intelligent labor, by a genius for enterprise, it has seen the country extend its intercourse and its influence to regions unknown to our fathers. Yet it has never abated one jot or tittle of the ancient law imposed on us by our God-fearing ancestors. We have fought a good fight, but also we have kept the faith. The Constitution of our fathers has been the light to our feet; our path is, and will ever remain, that of ordered progress, of liberty under the law. The country has vastly increased, but the great-brained statesmen who preceded us provided for infinite growth. The discoveries of science have made miraculous additions to our knowledge. But we are not daunted by progress; we are not afraid of the light. The fabric our fathers builded on such sure foundations will stand all shocks of fate or fortune. There will always be a proud pleasure in looking back on the history they made; but, guided by their example, the coming generation has the right to anticipate work not less important, days equally memorable to mankind. We who are passing off the stage bid you, as the children of Israel encamping by the sea were bidden, to Go Forward; we whose hands can no longer hold the flaming torch pass it on to you that its clear light may show the truth to the ages that are to come.

AMERICA'S LOVE OF PEACE

ADDRESS AT THIRTEENTH INTERNATIONAL CONGRESS OF PEACE
BOSTON, OCTOBER 3d, 1904

AMERICA'S LOVE OF PEACE

I ESTEEM it a great honor and privilege to be allowed to extend to you the welcome of the Government and the people of the United States of America on this memorable and auspicious occasion. No time could be more fitting for this gathering of a parliament of peace than to-day, when at the other end of the world the thunder of a destructive and sanguinary war is deafening the nations, while here we are preparing to settle the question of a vast transfer of power by an appeal to reason and orderly procedure, under the sanction of a law implicitly accepted by eighty millions of people.

And as if heaven had decided to give a sign of deepest significance to the hour of your meeting, it coincides with the commitment to eternal peace of all that was mortal of our dear and honored co-laborer in this sacred cause. George Frisbie Hoar had many titles to glory and honor. Not the least of them was the firm and constant courage with which, through all his illustrious life, he pleaded for humanity and universal good will.

No place could be more suitable than this high-hearted city, which has been for nearly three hundred years the birthplace and the home of every idea of progress and enlightenment which has germinated in the Western World. To bid you welcome to the home of Vane, of Winthrop, and of Adams, of Channing and Emerson, is to give you the freedom of no mean city, to make you partakers of a spiritual inheritance without which, with all our opulence, we should be poor indeed. It is true that this great Commonwealth has sought, with the sword, peace under liberty. We confess that many wars have left their traces in the pages of its history and its literature; art has adorned the public places of this stately town with the statues of its heroic sons. But the dominant note of its highest culture, its most persistent spirit, has been that righteousness which exalteth a nation, that obedience to the inner light which leads along the paths of peace.

And the policy of the nation at large, which owes so much of its civic spirit to the founders of New England, has been in the main a policy of peace. During the hundred and twenty years of our independent existence we have had but three wars with the outside world, though we have had a most grievous and dolorous struggle with our own people. We have had, I think, a greater relative immunity from war than any of our neighbors. All our greatest men have been earnest advocates of peace. The very men who founded our liberties with the mailed hand detested and abhorred war as the most futile and ferocious of human follies. Franklin and Jefferson repeatedly denounced it—the one with all the energy of his rhetoric, the other with the lambent fire of his wit. But not our philosophers alone—our fighting men have seen at close quarters how hideous is the face of war. Washington said, "My first wish is to see this plague to mankind banished from the earth"; and again he said, "We have experienced enough of its evils in this country to know that it should not be wantonly or unnecessarily entered upon." There is no discordant note in the utterances of our most eminent soldiers on this subject. The most famous utterance of General Grant—the one which will linger longest in the memories of men—was the prayer of his war-weary heart, "Let us have peace." Sherman reached the acme of his marvelous gift of epigram when he said, "War is hell." And Abraham Lincoln, after the four terrible years in which he had directed our vast armies and navies, uttered on the threshold of eternity the fervent and touching aspiration that "the mighty scourge of war might speedily pass away."

There has been no solution of continuity in the sentiments of our Presidents on this subject up to this day. McKinley deplored with every pulse of his honest and kindly heart the advent of the war which he had hoped might not come in his day, and gladly hailed the earliest moment for making peace; and President Roosevelt has the same tireless energy in the work of concord that he displayed when he sought peace and ensured it on the field of battle. No Presidents in our history have been so faithful and so efficient as the last two in the cause of arbitration and of every peaceful settlement of differences. I mention them together because their work has been harmonious and consistent. We hailed with joy the generous initiative of the Russian Emperor, and sent to the conference at The Hague the best men we had in our civic and military life. When The Hague Court lay apparently wrecked at the beginning of its voyage, threatened with death before it had fairly begun to live, it was the American Government which gave it the breath of life by inviting the Republic of Mexico to share our appeal to its jurisdiction; and the second case brought before it was at the instance of Mr. Roosevelt, who declined in its favor the high honor of arbitrating an affair of world-wide importance.

I beg you to believe, it is not by way of boasting that I recall these incidents to your minds; it is rather as a profession of faith in a cause which the present Administration has deeply at heart that I ask you to remember, in the deliberations upon which you are entering, the course to which the American Government is pledged and which it has steadily pursued for the last seven years. It is true that in those years we have had a hundred days of war—but they put an end forever to bloodshed which had lasted a generation. We landed a few platoons of marines on the Isthmus last year;

but that act closed without a shot a sanguinary succession of trivial wars. We marched a little army to Peking; but it was to save not only the beleaguered legations, but a great imperiled civilization. By mingled gentleness and energy, to which most of the world beyond our borders has done justice, we have given to the Philippines, if not peace, at least a nearer approach to it than they have had within the memory of men.

If our example is worth anything to the world, we have given it in the vital matter of disarmament. We have brought away from the Far East 55,000 soldiers whose work was done, and have sent them back to the fields of peaceful activity. We have reduced our Army to its minimum of 60,000 men; in fact, we may say we have no army, but in place of one a nucleus for drill and discipline. We have three-fourths of one soldier for every thousand of the population—a proportion which if adopted by other powers would at once eliminate wars and rumors of wars from the daily thoughts of the chancelleries of the world.

But fixed as our tradition is, clear as is our purpose in the direction of peace, no country is permanently immune to war so long as the desire and the practice of peace are not universal. If we quote Washington as an advocate of peace, it is but fair also to quote him where he says: "To be prepared for war is one of the most effectual means of preserving peace." And at another time he said: "To an active external commerce the protection of a naval force is indispensable. To secure respect to a neutral flag requires a naval force organized and ready to vindicate it from insult or aggression." To acknowledge the existence of an evil is not to support or approve it; but the facts must be faced. Human history is one long desolate story of bloodshed. All the arts unite in the apparent conspiracy to give precedence to the glory of arms. Demosthenes and Pericles adjured the Athenians by the memory of their battles. Horace boasted that he had been a soldier, *non sine gloria.* Even Milton, in that sublime sonnet where he said, "Peace hath her victories no less renowned than war," mentioned among the godly trophies of Cromwell "Darwen stream with blood of Scots imbrued." In almost every sermon and hymn we hear in our churches the imagery of war and battle is used. We are charged to fight the good fight of faith; we are to sail through bloody seas to win the prize. The Christian soldier is constantly marshaled to war. Not only in our habits and customs, but in our daily speech and in our inmost thoughts we are beset by the obsession of conflict and mutual destruction. It is like the law of sin in the members to which the greatest of the Apostles refers: "Who shall deliver us from the body of this death?"

I am speaking to those who recognize the lamentable state of things and who yet do not accept it, or submit to it, and who hope that through the shadow of this night we shall sweep into a younger day. How is this great deliverance to be accomplished?

We have all recently read that wonderful sermon on war by Count Tolstoi, in which a spirit of marvelous lucidity and fire, absolutely detached from geographical or political conditions, speaks the Word as it has been given him to speak it, and as no other living man could have done. As you read, with an aching heart, his terrible arraignment of war, feeling that as a man you are partly responsible for all human atrocities, you wait with impatience for the remedy he shall propose, and you find it is —Religion. Yes, that is the remedy. If all would do right, nobody would do wrong—nothing is plainer. It is a counsel of perfection, satisfactory to prophets and saints, to be reached in God's good time. But you are here to consult together to see whether the generation now alive may not do something to hasten the coming of the acceptable day, the appearance on earth of the beatific vision. If we can not at once make peace and good will the universal rule and practice of nations, what can we do to approximate this condition? What measures can we now take which may lead us at least a little distance toward the wished-for goal?

I have not come to advise you; I have no such ambitious pretensions. I do not even aspire to take part in your deliberations. But I am authorized to assure you that the American Government extends to you a cordial and sympathetic welcome, and shares to the utmost the spirit and purpose in which you have met. The President, so long as he remains in power, has no thought of departing from the traditions bequeathed us by the great soldiers and statesmen of our early history, which have been strictly followed during the last seven years. We shall continue to advocate and to carry into effect, as far as practicable, the principle of the arbitration of such questions as may not be settled through diplomatic negotiations. We have already done much in this direction; we shall hope to do much more. The President is now considering the negotiation of treaties of arbitration with such of the European powers as desire them, and hopes to lay them before the Senate next winter. And, finally, the President has only a few days ago promised, in response to the request of the Interparliamentary Union, to invite the nations to a second conference at The Hague to continue the beneficent work of the Conference of 1899.

Unhappily we can not foresee in the immediate future the cessation of wars upon the earth. We ought therefore to labor constantly for the mitigation of the horrors of war, especially to do what we can to lessen the sufferings of those who have no part in the struggle. This has been one of the most warmly cherished wishes of the last two Administrations. I make no apology for reading you a paragraph from the message which President Roosevelt sent to Congress last December.

There seems good ground for the belief that there has been a real growth among the civilized nations of a sentiment which will permit a gradual substitution of other methods than the method of war in the settlement of disputes. It is not pretended that as yet we are near a position in which it will be possible wholly to prevent war, or that a just regard for national interest and honor will in all cases permit of the settlement of international disputes by arbitration; but by a mixture of prudence and firmness with wisdom we think it is possible to do away with much of the provocation and excuse for war, and at least in many cases to substitute some other and more rational method for the settlement of disputes. The Hague Court offers so good an example of what can be done in the direction of such settlement that it should be encouraged in every way.

Further steps should be taken. In President McKinley's annual message of December 5, 1898, he made the following recommendation:

"The experiences of the last year bring forcibly home to us a sense of the burdens and the waste of war. We desire, in common with most civilized nations, to reduce to the lowest possible point the damage sustained in time of war by peaceable trade and commerce. It is true we may suffer in such cases less than other communities, but all nations are damaged more or less by the state of uneasiness and apprehension into which an outbreak of hostilities throws the entire commercial world. It should be our object, therefore, to minimize, so far as practicable, this inevitable loss and disturbance. This purpose can probably best be accomplished by an international agreement to regard all private property at sea as exempt from capture or destruction by the forces of belligerent powers. The United States Government has for many years advocated this humane and beneficent principle, and is now in a position to recommend it to other powers without the imputation of selfish motives. I therefore suggest for your consideration that the Executive be authorized to correspond with the governments of the principal maritime powers with a view of incorporating into the permanent law of civilized nations the principle of the exemption of all private property at sea, not contraband of war, from capture or destruction by belligerent powers."

The President urged this beneficent scheme with an earnestness which gained the willing attention of Congress, already predisposed to it in spirit, and on the 28th of April of this year he was able to approve a joint resolution of both Houses recommending that the "President endeavor to bring about an understanding among the principal maritime powers with a view of incorporating into the permanent law of civilized nations the principle of the exemption of all private property at sea, not contraband of war, from capture or destruction by belligerents."

It has not been thought advisable by the President during the past summer to call the attention of the powers to a project which would necessarily be regarded by two of them, and possibly by others, with reference to its bearing upon the deplorable conflict now raging in the Far East. But as we earnestly pray that the return of peace may not be long delayed between the two nations, to both of which we are bound by so many historic ties, we may confidently look forward at no distant day to inviting the attention of the nations to this matter, and we hope we may have the powerful influence of this great organization in gaining their adherence.

The time allotted to me is at an end. I can only bid you Godspeed in your work. The task you have set yourselves, the purpose to which you are devoted, have won the praise of earth and the blessing of Heaven since the morning of time. The noblest of all the beatitudes is the consecration promised the peacemakers. Even if in our time we may not win the wreath of olive; even if we may not hear the golden clamor of the trumpets celebrating the reign of universal and enduring peace, it is something to have desired it, to have worked for it in the measure of our forces. And if you now reap no visible guerdon of your labors the peace of God that passes understanding will be your all-sufficient reward.

LIFE IN THE WHITE HOUSE IN THE TIME OF LINCOLN

FROM "THE CENTURY MAGAZINE" FOR NOVEMBER, 1890

LIFE IN THE WHITE HOUSE IN THE TIME OF LINCOLN

THE daily life of the White House during the momentous years of Lincoln's presidency had a character of its own, different from that of any previous or subsequent time. In the first days after the inauguration there was the unprecedented rush of office-seekers, inspired by a strange mixture of enthusiasm and greed, pushed by motives which were perhaps at bottom selfish, but which had nevertheless a curious touch of that deep emotion which had stirred the heart of the nation in the late election. They were not all ignoble; among that dense crowd that swarmed in the staircases and the corridors there were many well-to-do men who were seeking office to their own evident damage, simply because they wished to be a part, however humble, of a government which they had aided to put in power and to which they were sincerely devoted. Many of the visitors who presented so piteous a figure in those early days of 1861 afterwards marched, with the independent dignity of a private soldier, in the ranks of the Union Army, or rode at the head of their regiments like men born to command. There were few who had not a story worth listening to, if there were time and opportunity. But the numbers were so great, the competition was so keen, that they ceased for the moment to be regarded as individuals, drowned as they were in the general sea of solicitation.

Few of them received office; when, after weeks of waiting, one of them got access to the President, he was received with kindness by a tall, melancholy-looking man sitting at a desk with his back to a window which opened upon a fair view of the Potomac, who heard his story with a gentle patience, took his papers and referred them to one of the Departments, and that was all; the fatal pigeon-holes devoured them. As time wore on and the offices were filled the throng of eager aspirants diminished and faded away. When the war burst out an immediate transformation took place. The house was again invaded and overrun by a different class of visitors—youths who wanted commissions in the regulars; men who wished to raise irregular regiments or battalions without regard to their State authorities; men who wanted to furnish stores to the army; inventors full of great ideas and in despair at the apathy of the world; later, an endless stream of officers in search of promotion or desirable assignments. And from first to last there were the politicians and statesmen in Congress and out, each of whom felt that he had the right by virtue of his representative capacity to as much of the President's time as he chose, and who never considered that he and his kind were many and that the President was but one.

It would be hard to imagine a state of things less conducive to serious and effective work, yet in one way or another the work was done. In the midst of a crowd of visitors who began to arrive early in the morning and who were put out, grumbling, by the servants who closed the doors at midnight, the President pursued those labors which will carry his name to distant ages. There was little order or system about it; those around him strove from beginning to end to erect barriers to defend him against constant interruption, but the President himself was always the first to break them down. He disliked anything that kept people from him who wanted to see him, and although the continual contact with importunity which he could not satisfy, and with distress which he could not always relieve, wore terribly upon him and made him an old man before his time, he would never take the necessary measures to defend himself. He continued to the end receiving these swarms of visitors, every one of whom, even the most welcome, took something from him in the way of wasted nervous force. Henry Wilson once remonstrated with him about it: "You will wear yourself out." He replied, with one of those smiles in which there was so much of sadness, "They don't want much; they get but little, and I must see them." In most cases he could do them no good, and it afflicted him to see he could not make them understand the impossibility of granting their requests. One hot afternoon a private soldier who had somehow got access to him persisted, after repeated explanation that his case was one to be settled by his immediate superiors, in begging that the President would give it his personal attention. Lincoln at last burst out: "Now, my man, go away! I cannot attend to all these details. I could as easily bail out the Potomac with a spoon."

Of course it was not all pure waste; Mr. Lincoln gained much of information, something of cheer and encouragement, from these visits. He particularly enjoyed conversing with officers of the army and navy, newly arrived from the field or from sea. He listened with the eagerness of a child over a fairy tale to Garfield's graphic account of the battle of Chickamauga; he was always delighted with the wise and witty sailor talk of John A. Dahlgren, Gustavus V. Fox, and Commander Henry A. Wise. Sometimes a word fitly spoken had its results. When R. B. Ayres called on him in company with Senator Harris, and was introduced as a captain of artillery who had taken part in a recent unsuccessful engagement, he asked, "How many guns did you take in?" "Six," Ayres answered. "How many did you bring out?" the President asked, maliciously. "Eight." This unexpected reply did much to gain Ayres his merited promotion.

The President rose early, as his sleep was

light and capricious. In the summer, when he lived at the Soldiers' Home, he would take his frugal breakfast and ride into town in time to be at his desk at eight o'clock. He began to receive visits nominally at ten o'clock, but long before that hour struck the doors were besieged by anxious crowds, through whom the people of importance, senators and members of Congress, elbowed their way after the fashion which still survives. On days when the Cabinet met, Tuesdays and Fridays, the hour of noon closed the interviews of the morning. On other days it was the President's custom, at about that hour, to order the doors to be opened and all who were waiting to be admitted. The crowd would rush in, thronging the narrow room, and one by one would make their wants known. Some came merely to shake hands, to wish him Godspeed; their errand was soon done. Others came asking help or mercy; they usually pressed forward, careless, in their pain, as to what ears should overhear their prayer. But there were many who lingered in the rear and leaned against the wall, hoping each to be the last, that they might in tête-à-tête unfold their schemes for their own advantage or their neighbors' hurt. These were often disconcerted by the President's loud and hearty, "Well, friend, what can I do for you?" which compelled them to speak, or retire and wait for a more convenient season.

The inventors were more a source of amusement than annoyance. They were usually men of some originality of character, not infrequently carried to eccentricity. Lincoln had a quick comprehension of mechanical principles, and often detected a flaw in an invention which the contriver had overlooked. He would sometimes go out into the waste fields that then lay south of the Executive Mansion to test an experimental gun or torpedo. He used to quote with much merriment the solemn dictum of one rural inventor that "a gun ought not to rekyle; if it rekyled at all, it ought to rekyle a little forrid." He was particularly interested in the first rude attempts at the afterwards famous mitrailleuses; on one occasion he worked one with his own hands at the Arsenal, and sent forth peals of Homeric laughter as the balls, which had not power to penetrate the target set up at a little distance, came bounding back among the shins of the bystanders. He accompanied Colonel Hiram Berdan one day to the camp of his sharpshooters and there practised in the trenches his long-disused skill with the rifle. A few fortunate shots from his own gun and his pleasure at the still better marksmanship of Berdan led to the arming of that admirable regiment with breech-loaders.

At luncheon time he had literally to run the gantlet through the crowds who filled the corridors between his office and the rooms at the west end of the house occupied by the family. The afternoon wore away in much the same manner as the morning; late in the day he usually drove out for an hour's airing; at six o'clock he dined. He was one of the most abstemious of men; the pleasures of the table had few attractions for him. His breakfast was an egg and a cup of coffee; at luncheon he rarely took more than a biscuit and a glass of milk, a plate of fruit in its season; at dinner he ate sparingly of one or two courses. He drank little or no wine; not that he remained always on principle a total abstainer, as he was during a part of his early life in the fervor of the "Washingtonian" reform; but he never cared for wine or liquors of any sort, and never used tobacco.

LIFE IN THE WHITE HOUSE

There was little gaiety in the Executive house during his time. It was an epoch, if not of gloom, at least of a seriousness too intense to leave room for much mirth. There were the usual formal entertainments, the traditional state dinners and receptions, conducted very much as they have been ever since. The great public receptions, with their vast rushing multitudes pouring past him to shake hands, he rather enjoyed; they were not a disagreeable task to him, and he seemed surprised when people commiserated him upon them. He would shake hands with thousands of people, seemingly unconscious of what he was doing, murmuring some monotonous salutation as they went by, his eye dim, his thoughts far withdrawn; then suddenly he would see some familiar face,—his memory for faces was very good,—and his eye would brighten and his whole form grow attentive; he would greet the visitor with a hearty grasp and a ringing word and dismiss him with a cheery laugh that filled the Blue Room with infectious good nature. Many people armed themselves with an appropriate speech to be delivered on these occasions, but unless it was compressed into the smallest possible space it never got utterance; the crowd would jostle the peroration out of shape. If it were brief enough and hit the President's fancy, it generally received a swift answer. One night an elderly gentleman from Buffalo said, "Up our way, we believe in God and Abraham Lincoln," to which the President replied, shoving him along the line, "My friend, you are more than half right."

During the first year of the administration the house was made lively by the games and pranks of Mr. Lincoln's two younger children, William and Thomas: Robert, the eldest, was away at Harvard, only coming home for short vacations. The two little boys, aged eight and ten, with their Western independence and enterprise, kept the house in an uproar. They drove their tutor wild with their good-natured disobedience; they organized a minstrel show in the attic; they made acquaintance with the office-seekers and became the hot champions of the distressed. William was, with all his boyish frolic, a child of great promise, capable of close application and study. He had a fancy for drawing up railway time-tables, and would conduct an imaginary train from Chicago to New York with perfect precision. He wrote childish verses, which sometimes attained the unmerited honors of print. But this bright, gentle, studious child sickened and died in February, 1862. His father was profoundly moved by his death, though he gave no outward sign of his trouble, but kept about his work the same as ever. His bereaved heart seemed afterwards to pour out its fullness on his youngest child. "Tad" was a merry, warm-blooded, kindly little boy, perfectly lawless, and full of odd fancies and inventions, the "chartered libertine" of the Executive Mansion. He ran continually in and out of his father's cabinet, interrupting his gravest labors and conversations with his bright, rapid, and very imperfect speech—for he had an impediment which made his articulation almost unintelligible until he was nearly grown. He would perch upon his father's knee, and sometimes even on his shoulder, while the most weighty conferences were going on. Sometimes escaping from the domestic authorities, he would take refuge in that sanctuary for the whole evening, dropping to sleep at last on the floor, when the President would pick him up and carry him tenderly to bed.

Mr. Lincoln's life was almost devoid of recreation. He sometimes went to the theater, and was particularly fond of a play of Shakspere's well acted. He was so delighted with Hackett in *Falstaff* that he wrote him a letter of warm congratulation which pleased the veteran actor so much that he gave it to the "New York Herald," which printed it with abusive comments. Hackett was greatly mortified and made suitable apologies; upon which the President wrote to him again in the kindliest manner, saying:

> Give yourself no uneasiness on the subject. . . . I certainly did not expect to see my note in print; yet I have not been much shocked by the comments upon it. They are a fair specimen of what has occurred to me through life. I have endured a great deal of ridicule, without much malice; and have received a great deal of kindness, not quite free from ridicule. I am used to it.

This incident had the usual sequel: the veteran comedian asked for an office, which the President was not able to give him, and the pleasant acquaintance ceased. A hundred times this experience was repeated: a man whose disposition and talk were agreeable would be introduced to the President; he took pleasure in his conversation for two or three interviews, and then this congenial person would ask some favor impossible to grant, and go away in bitterness of spirit. It is a cross that every President must bear.

Mr. Lincoln spent most of his evenings in his office, though occasionally he remained in the drawing-room after dinner, conversing with visitors or listening to music, for which he had an especial liking, though he was not versed in the science, and preferred simple ballads to more elaborate compositions. In his office he was not often suffered to be alone; he frequently passed the evening there with a few friends in frank and free conversation. If the company was all of one sort he was at his best; his wit and rich humor had free play; he was once more the Lincoln of the Eighth Circuit, the cheeriest of talkers, the riskiest of story tellers; but if a stranger came in he put on in an instant his whole armor of dignity and reserve. He had a singular discernment of men; he would talk of the most important political and military concerns with a freedom which often amazed his intimates, but we do not recall an instance in which this confidence was misplaced.

Where only one or two were present he was fond of reading aloud. He passed many of the summer evenings in this way when occupying his cottage at the Soldiers' Home. He would there read Shakespere for hours with a single secretary for audience. The plays he most affected were "Hamlet," "Macbeth," and the series of Histories; among these he never tired of "Richard II." The terrible outburst of grief and despair into which *Richard* falls in the third act had a peculiar fascination for him. I have heard him read it at Springfield, at the White House, and at the Soldiers' Home.

For heaven's sake, let us sit upon the ground,
And tell sad stories of the death of kings:—
How some have been deposed, some slain in war,
Some haunted by the ghosts they have deposed;
Some poisoned by their wives, some sleeping killed;
All murdered:—For within the hollow crown
That rounds the mortal temples of a king
Keeps Death his court; and there the antic sits,
Scoffing his state, and grinning at his pomp,—
Allowing him a breath, a little scene
To monarchize, be feared, and kill with looks;
Infusing him with self and vain conceit,—

As if this flesh, which walls about our life,
Were brass impregnable,—and humored thus,
Comes at the last, and with a little pin
Bores through his castle walls and—farewell, King!

He read Shakespere more than all other writers together. He made no attempt to keep pace with the ordinary literature of the day. Sometimes he read a scientific work with keen appreciation, but he pursued no systematic course. He owed less to reading than most men. He delighted in Burns; he said one day after reading those exquisite lines to Glencairn, beginning, "The bridegroom may forget the bride," that "Burns never touched a sentiment without carrying it to its ultimate expression and leaving nothing further to be said." Of Thomas Hood he was also excessively fond. He often read aloud "The Haunted House." He would go to bed with a volume of Hood in his hands, and would sometimes rise at midnight and traversing the long halls of the Executive Mansion in his night clothes would come to his secretary's room and read aloud something that especially pleased him. He wanted to share his enjoyment of the writer; it was dull pleasure to him to laugh alone. He read Bryant and Whittier with appreciation; there were many poems of Holmes's that he read with intense relish. "The Last Leaf" was one of his favorites; he knew it by heart, and used often to repeat with deep feeling:

> The mossy marbles rest
> On the lips that he has pressed
> In their bloom;
> And the names he loved to hear
> Have been carved for many a year
> On the tomb;

giving the marked Southwestern pronunciation of the words "hear" and "year." A poem by William Knox, "Oh, why should the Spirit of Mortal be proud?" he learned by heart in his youth, and used to repeat all his life.

Upon all but two classes the President made the impression of unusual power as well as of unusual goodness. He failed only in the case of those who judged men by a purely conventional standard of breeding, and upon those so poisoned by political hostility that the testimony of their own eyes and ears became untrustworthy. He excited no emotion but one of contempt in the finely tempered mind of Hawthorne; several English tourists have given the most distorted pictures of his speech and his manners. Some Southern writers who met him in the first days of 1861 spoke of him as a drunken, brawling boor, whose mouth dripped with oaths and tobacco, when in truth whisky and tobacco were as alien to his lips as profanity. There is a story current in England, as on the authority of the late Lord Lyons, on the coarse jocularity with which he once received a formal diplomatic communication; but as Lord Lyons told the story there was nothing objectionable about it. The British Minister called at the White House to announce the marriage of the Prince of Wales. He made the formal speech appropriate to the occasion; the President replied in the usual conventional manner. The requisite formalities having thus been executed, the President took the bachelor diplomatist by the hand, saying, "And now, Lord Lyons, go thou and do likewise."

The evidence of all the men admitted to his intimacy is that he maintained, without the least effort or assumption, a singular dignity and reserve in the midst of his easiest conversation. Charles A. Dana says, "Even in his freest moments one always felt the presence of a will and an intellectual power which maintained the ascendancy of the President." In his relations to his Cabinet "it was always plain that he was the master and they were the subordinates. They constantly had to yield to his will, and if he ever yielded to them it was because they convinced him that the course they advised was judicious and appropriate." While men of the highest culture and position thus recognized his intellectual primacy there was no man so humble as to feel abashed before him. Frederick Douglass beautifully expressed the sentiment of the plain people in his company: "I feel as though I was in the presence of a big brother and that there was safety in his atmosphere."

As time wore on and the war held its terrible course, upon no one of all those who lived through it were its effects more apparent than upon the President. He bore the sorrows of the nation in his own heart; he suffered deeply not only from disappointments, from treachery, from hope deferred, from the open assaults of enemies, and from the sincere anger of discontented friends, but also from the world-wide distress and affliction which flowed from the great conflict in which he was engaged and which he could not evade. One of the most tender and compassionate of men, he was forced to give orders which cost thousands of lives; by nature a man of order and thrift, he saw the daily spectacle of unutterable waste and destruction which he could not prevent. The cry of the widow and the orphan was always in his ears; the awful responsibility resting upon him as the protector of an imperiled republic kept him true to his duty, but could not make him unmindful of the intimate details of that vast sum of human misery involved in a civil war.

Under this frightful ordeal his demeanor and disposition changed—so gradually that it would be impossible to say when the change began; but he was in mind, body, and nerves a very different man at the second inauguration from the one who had taken the oath in 1861. He continued always the same kindly, genial, and cordial spirit he had been at first; but the boisterous laughter became less frequent year by year; the eye grew veiled by constant meditation on momentous subjects; the air of reserve and detachment from his surroundings increased. He aged with great rapidity.

This change is shown with startling distinctness by two life-masks—the one made by Leonard W. Volk in Chicago, April, 1860, the other by Clark Mills in Washington, in the spring of 1865. The first is of a man of fifty-one, and young for his years. The face has a clean, firm outline; it is free from fat, but the muscles are hard and full; the large mobile mouth is ready to speak, to shout, or laugh; the bold, curved nose is broad and substantial, with spreading nostrils; it is a face full of life, of energy, of vivid aspiration. The other is so sad and peaceful in its infinite repose that the famous sculptor Augustus Saint-Gaudens insisted, when he first saw it, that it was a death-mask. The lines are set, as if the living face, like the copy, had been in bronze; the nose is thin, and lengthened by the emaciation of the cheeks; the mouth is fixed like that of an archaic statue; a look as of one on whom sorrow and care had done their worst without victory is on all the features; the whole expression is of unspeakable sadness and all-sufficing strength. Yet the peace is not the dreadful peace of death; it is the peace that passeth understanding.

CLARENCE KING

FROM THE "CLARENCE KING" MEMOIRS PUBLISHED FOR THE CENTURY ASSOCIATION

CLARENCE KING

WE sometimes, though most rarely, meet a man of a nature so genial, of qualities so radiant, so instinct with vitality, that in connection with him the thought of mortality seems incongruous. Such men appear as exempt from the ordinary lethal fate of the rest of us as the "happy gods" of the Greek poets. They are not necessarily fortunate or prosperous, but whatever their luck or their accidents they seem as independent of them as actors are of their momentary disguises. The law of their nature is to be radiant; clouds are to them a transient and negligible condition. While they live they are surrounded by an atmosphere of universal regard and admiration, and when the end comes, though the mourning of their friends is deep and sincere, it is tinged with something exquisite and splendid, like the luxury of purple and gold that attends the close of a troubled and electric day.

Such a man was Clarence King. While he lived, it was our habit to believe that no real evil could befall him; and now that he is dead, —although we know we have lost something from life which made it especially precious and desirable, yet there remains a souvenir so delightful, so filled with tenderness and inspiration, that there are few pleasures the world contains so valuable as his memory in the hearts of his friends.

He possessed to an extraordinary degree the power of attracting and attaching to himself friends of every sort and condition. The cowboys and packers of the plains and the hills; the employes of railroads and hotels; men of science and men of commerce; the Senate and the clergy—in all these ways of life his friends were numerous and devoted, bound to him by a singular sympathy and mutual comprehension. When in middle life —if we may use this expression in reference to one who was always young—he went to Europe, he continued the same facile conquest of hearts. In this he was aided by a remarkable ease in acquiring a colloquial command of languages. Having occasion to go to Mexico, he put in his pocket a small Spanish Dictionary and without the aid of a Grammar got by heart some thousand nouns and verbs in the infinitive, so that on arriving at Guaymas he was master of a highly effective and picturesque jargon which delighted the Mexicans and carried him triumphantly to the mines of Culiacan. Afterwards he acquired a correct and grammatical knowledge of the Castilian. It was the same in France. He had read French from childhood, but had never spoken it. On arriving in Paris, where he was conducting some important business, he did not pause to gain familiarity with the spoken idiom. He attacked it with the energy of a cavalry charge, and though at first he made havoc of genders, moods and tenses, he took it as we are told the Kingdom of Heaven is taken, by violence. In a few weeks he was speaking the language with perfect ease, and was an equally welcome guest in financial, artistic and literary circles. In England nothing describes his success but the well-worn phrase of Dickens. He was "the delight of the nobility and gentry" and not of them only, but he made friends also in Whitechapel and Soho, and even to some in the submerged fraction, the most wretched derelicts of civilization, he brought the ineffable light of his keen comprehension and generous sympathy. I introduced him once to a woman of eminent distinction, one of the first writers of our time. Afer he had gone, she said: "I understand now the secret of his charm. It is his kindness."

It is not for me to speak of his commanding place in the world of science: his associates and colleagues will keep that phase of his life in remembrance. I think his reputation as a great physicist suffered somewhat from the dazzling attractiveness of his personality. It was hard to remember that this polished trifler, this exquisite wit, who diffused over every conversation in which he was engaged an iridescent mist of epigram and persiflage, was one of the greatest savants of his time. It was hard to take seriously a man who was so deliciously agreeable. Yet his work on Systematic Geology is a masterpiece of practical and ordered learning, and his treatise on The

Age of the Earth has been accepted as the profoundest and most authoritative utterance on the subject yet made.

If he had given himself to literature, he would have been a great writer. The range of his knowledge, both of man and nature, was enormous; his sympathy was universal; his mastery of the word, his power of phrase, was almost unlimited. His literary product is considerable and will keep his name alive; but it bears no appreciable proportion to the literary treasures he squandered in his daily and nightly conversation. I recall, with the sharpest regret of my own incapacity of memory, the evenings by my fireside, when he poured out in inexhaustible profusion his stores of fancy and invention. There were scores of short stories full of color and life, sketches of thrilling adventure, not less than half a dozen complete novels, boldly planned and brilliantly wrought out,—all ready for the type or the pen; which now—an infinite pity!—are only of the stuff that dreams are made of.

Few men had so quick and so sure an eye for art. In that first visit to Europe, to which I have alluded, he seemed like one to whom all the scenes he visited had been familiar in some antecedent state. His time was limited, and his pace, therefore, amazingly rapid. He swept through Spain like a breeze. He had apparently no preferences. In the space of a few weeks, he covered the whole field; he knew the masterpieces of classic and modern painting; he was familiar with the syncopated melodies of Cuba and Malaga and Andalusia; he was an *aficionado* in fans, embroideries and bronzes. Nobody has felt more keenly the melancholy charm of Castile; the proof is in that exquisite idyll of the Helmet of Mambrino. Fastidious as he was, he was yet easily pleased by whatever was natural and genuine. I remember his horror—in the midst of his enthusiasm over Spain—at meeting an eminent man of letters from New England who had found nothing in the Peninsula to suit him, and who wound up by expressing his disgust that "from Salamanca to Cadiz you could not get a fishball."

All over Europe he scampered with the same vertiginous speed, and the same serene and genial appearance of leisure, and perfect satisfaction and delight with all he saw. The art of Holland was as enchanting to him as that of Spain and Italy. His admiration of the great men of the past never rendered him unjust to the men of the present. His wide sympathies comprehended Velasquez and Fortuny in a kindred appreciation. He became at sight the friend of Mesdag and Israels. I took him to the studio of Gustave Doré, and in five minutes they were brothers and were planning an excursion to Arizona to sketch the war dances of the Apaches. A few days later the robust Alsatian, who seemed built to last a hundred years, was dead, stricken down by the terrible pneumonia of those years.

In England, while as I have said his success was universal with all classes, his closet intimacies were with men who were occupied with the things of the spirit. Ruskin took him to his heart, entertained him at Coniston, and offered him his choice of his two greatest water-colors by Turner. "One good Turner," said King, "deserves another," and took both.

Few men ever can have lived who loved knowingly and ardently so many things. All the arts gave him joy; his mind was hospitable to every intellectual delight, the simplest as well as the most complex. In music he enjoyed Beethoven and the latest rag-time; in painting he reveled in the masterpieces of all the schools; in poetry his taste was as keen as it was catholic; in literature he liked all styles except the tiresome; for years he read a chapter of higher mathematics every night before going to bed. He had the passionate love of nature which only the highest culture gives—the sky, the rock, and the river spoke to him as familiar friends.

I imagine that in comparing our impressions of him, the thought which comes uppermost in the minds of all of us, is that Clarence King resembled no one else whom we have ever known. The rest of our friends we divide into classes; King belonged to a class of his own. He was inimitable in many ways: in his inexhaustible fund of wise and witty speech; in his learning about which his marvelous humor played like summer lightning over far horizons; in his quick and intelligent sympathy which saw the good and the amusing in the most unpromising subjects; in the ease and the airy lightness with which he scattered his jeweled phrases; but above all in his astonishing power of diffusing happiness wherever he went. Years ago, in a well-known drawing room in Washington, when we were mourning his departure from the Capital, one of his friends expressed the opinion of all when he said, "It is strange that the Creator, when it would have been so easy to make more Kings, should have made only one."